Introduction

Frank Worsdale was a school boy during the difficult years of WWII. He was born in Rossington, a medium sized, Sou community. Luckily for us he kept this simpl and goings', providing us with a fascinating i village life during the war.

CW00449848

Many things that my children now take for g to young Frank. He talks about days when bananas arrive in the village and how his entire family took one bite each. He writes about his trips to the picture house, the films he saw, and the buses he caught. He tells us of his family Christmases, his siblings, illnesses, civic celebrations, and sad losses.

All in all, this book gives a through the key-hole view of one South Yorkshire family from well over sixty years ago. - **Symeon Waller, Doncaster History.**

DONCASTER HISTORY

www.doncasterhistory.co.uk

©Doncaster History Publishing 2012

A Rossington Schoolboy's WWII Diaries, 1944 & 1946

Jan 1st

- Let the New Year in.

Jan 2nd

- Nelly Spencer came to our house.

Jan 3rd

- Planted out 2 rows of spuds, 2 rows of peas, 1 row of beet, 1 row of carrots, and a patch of onions

Jan 5th

- Wireless talk on a conference in London on beverage report and planning after the war (2000 children were there)

Jan 6th

- Metal work at school.

Jan 9th

- Mary Worsdale's Birthday, aged 40.

Jan 10th

- At little bit of snow last night but gone by end of day.

Jan 11th

- A bit more snow and a bit of rain in the daytime, don't expect any more.

Jan 12th

- Lads in class 3A as follows: Tomlinson*, Keith Sanderson*, Conncanon, King*, Bows, Hughes, Ball, Haynes*, Leek, Robins, Green, Wood, Hart, Harris, Cinders*, Moody, Webber, Kilcorn, Adcock, Backer*, Pinder, Hallet, Sarson, Watson, Scarbrough*, Blount,

Tomson, Perry, Birchall, Loughlin, Robson*, Briggs, Espin. - *= summer boys who will leave at Easter.

Jan 15th
- My headline book – Bill, Frank, Mam, Dad, Raymond, and baby Peggy.

Jan 16th
- Joe Pine's birthday age 22.

Jan 17th
- Russians start new front near Leningrad. Advance of up to 12½ miles. Waste paper day.

Jan 18th
- Mr Churchill returns to England from illness in Tunisia, he went straight into parliament.

Jan 19th
- Morning wireless talk on weather. Learned in Science how weather bells work. Waste paper day.

Jan 20th
- Brought Boeing Fortress home from school, price 8d. A lot of slides this morning. Started Spitfire.

Jan 21st
- Dog bit me! Finished my book at school. Started black arrow. Allies land 30 miles from south of Rome. Nettuno is captured.

Jan 23rd
- Found a balloon today! First one I've seen since war began.

Jan 24th
- New landing forces deep inside Germany.

Jan 25th
- The town and airport of Littoria falls to allied army's 11 miles east of Nettuno.

Jan 26th
- Current affairs talk in school called 'Life in Denmark'. Bill fainted in school from singing! Advance in Italy, a small town is captured.

Jan 27th

- Oranges in Rossington, first for a few months, queue from Moxon's shop to Guests. In woodwork I worked on my spitfire and in metalwork I did my toasting fork.

Jan 28th

- Mr Eden, the foreign minister warns the Jap's about treating prisoners cruelly. They bayoneted some soldiers in their backs and tortured some others

Jan 29th

- Received 'Dig For Victory' leaflets. Russians on outskirts of Kirsk. Rosso' school football match with central 3-3 draw.

Jan 30th

- 2,000 bombers blast Frankfurt. London's 701st raid, not a very big one. Roosevelt's birthday today.

Jan 31st

- Had letter from Roy (best one yet!) Another 1,500 tons on Berlin. Aunt Becca went to the Panto, without Bill!

1st Feb

- New Bridgehead drive begins. Our class got 100 pc top. Ella helped Keith to dig garden over.

2nd Feb

- Air raid practice. Had bad back. Wireless talk at school on why Argentina broke off from Germany. Gap torn in Gustav line 15 miles from Rome.

3rd Feb

- Finished Spitfire at school. 1,100 planes bomb Wilhelm's haven. Allies are within 500 yds of Cassino. Rome can hear the allies guns.

4th Feb

- Got a bit of luck today, Mr Tagg gave us a change we had been waiting for, for over a year. Another trap closing on Nazis.

5th Feb

- Flitted into 9 Firth Crescent. Mr Fielding got the gas going for us, (don't think much of it up to press). Stiff fighting for Cassino.

6th Feb

- Russians tighten trap on Mansten. Hardly had any sleep last night.

7th Feb

- Nikopol escape. Gap closing for Nazis. Film show at school about the making of glass, and Ford cars.

8th Feb

- Keith Sanderson's birthday – age 14. Expected Peg home but she's not home. Nazis backtracking towards Kherson.

9th Feb

- Nikopol falls! Went upstairs in pictures for first time. Wireless talk on Mars and Americans.

10th Feb

- In woodwork I started mustang for Peg. Russian strength crowds on Krivolrog.

11th Feb

- Got new house tidied up now. Bombers back up fifth army. Fighting in Italy still going slow. Not much news from new front.

12th Feb
- Peggy took me to Doncaster. Got 4 sandwiches and 2 cups of Bonvita which cost 1/10. Fifth army beats off new attacks.

13th Feb
- Slept in new bed. Had game of cricket last night, first in 1944. Rome will be won says Churchill.

14th Feb
- School team beat Edlington 3-1, Forest and Sarson scored. British troops advance, shelling Cassino.

15th Feb
- Took my boots to cobblers (size 7, brown).Australian apples at a few shops. 100 flying fortresses bomb Germans in Italy.

16th Feb
- Wireless talk at school about submarines and the food the crew eat etc. They get good food. Berlin gets 2,500 tons of bombs dropped on them. 45 planes lost out of 1,000.

17th Feb
- Peg went back. Had to stop off school in afternoon as boots still not ready. Started Maran fighter in woodwork. New Anzio battle begins.

18th Feb
- An American ship sunk, 1,000 soldiers drowned. Got some apples (Australian) only 8½ d. Nazis driven from Russia.

19th Feb
- Got small bottle of dark oak stain, smallest in shop 1/-, Bill got some new stocking, plain 1/1½ okay. Shimsk falls to Russians 250 yds from Cassino Abbey, they say they'll have it in 24 hours.

20th Feb
- Patched my pants, at least stitched an old patch on.

21st Feb
- Pantomime on at church hall 1/- or 1/6. Football at school. Largest air raid yet. 126 German planes shot down 100 of ours. Stuttgart was the main target last night with 2,000 planes.

22ⁿᵈ Feb

- Had football for highest attendance. Had some pancakes but no lemon or orange juice. Bill got bit by dog. We have lost 45 war ships since Jan 1ˢᵗ. Mr Churchill says U-boats are being defeated.

23ʳᵈ Feb

- Finland, Bulgaria, Hungary, Romania are with Germany because they thought they'd win. America shot down 310 planes in 3 days.

24ᵗʰ Feb

- Mrs Metham to old village church which is 802 years old.

25ᵗʰ Feb

- Brought aeroplane downstairs, it was not out 2 minutes until it was broke. Got entrance from for tech school. Rogachev taken in new offensive.

26ᵗʰ Feb

- Went to see film show at church hall 6d. Took legs off drawers.

27ᵗʰ Feb

- Snow about 4" deep, snowed all day. Blitz reaches new fury.

28ᵗʰ Feb

- Had some pancakes for dinner. Snow still here. Bus crashes near Balby, killing 1 person.

29ᵗʰ Feb

- Broke up from school today. Stood in fish shop queue for 1½ hours. Germans new attack tries to drive allies into sea.

1st Mar

- Batch of oranges in Rosso, people waiting from ½ past 12 until 4. Bulgaria reported asking for peace terms.

2nd Mar

- Got wood from Guest's for gate, 4 planks for 1/-, got lads to pull them home on sledges. Augusburg again bombed heavily.

3rd Mar

- Went to Joyce Griffith's birthday party. Park turned into fields with piles of manure all over. Raids on Germany and France today.

4th Mar

- Mum got a lemon. Went to tech school for exam, results in a few weeks. A bit more snow but rained after. Great Air Armada out again today.

5th Mar

- Noose on Askov is tightening. First seeds this year – shooting cress. Berlin bombed again by 14 bombers and 26 fighters.

6th Mar

- Uncle Charles' birthday. Had an orange to eat on way to school, first for a long time. Toffee coupons started. Berlin bombed again, 176 nz shot 1.

7th Mar

- Film show at school about Bakelite plastics. Had pancakes for tea. Pit strikes spread! Navy ready for new offensive.

8th Mar

- Wireless talk at school about ferrous, alloys, chrome, nickel, etc and saw how machine gun works. Made a stool from a box. Germany heavily raided today.

9th Mar

- Went to Scarbrough barracks to see 'dig for victory' exhibition in morning then dug some garden over. Berlin has another big raid (124 js??) got 17.

10th Mar

- We've had 58 oranges in our ward since January.

11th Mar.

- Got 2/- off Aunt for digging her garden over and 6d off Mrs Debman for going to the fish shop.

12th Mar

- Ice cream in Doncaster yesterday, 2d measure for 1/-. Went to church. Nazis are reeling back in Ukraine. Not much news from Italy. Casino is not captured yet even though 5 weeks ago they were 500 yds from it!!

13th Mar

- Got some lemons from Munson's (1Lb), second time since beginning of war. Keith got his employment card. Many miners go back to work.

14th Mar

- Sold 1 book of tickets with Keith. Got top shield at school. Dad and I fixed gate on. Eire will be isolated says Churchill.

15th Mar

- Wireless talk on Switzerland, it is home of Red Cross, they are on no-one's side. New blows on central Reich.

16th Mar

- Started Boston in woodwork, did nothing to my toast fork. Over 3,000 tons of bombs on Stuttgart. Sung at school by myself.

17th Mar

- Went to boys club. Ray had dinner at pit. Dorothy Elliott gets 6 years for stealing £100,000!

18th Mar

- Made my second stool for Aunt out of old boxes. Went to pictures for 2½ hours. Allies take Casino station.

19th Mar

- Got another brother at ½ past 1 this morning, 7½ lbs. Pauline Johnston came to house after church. Russians smash another German army.

20th Mar

- Britain has got 12,000lb bomb, biggest ever!! Had to look after house, Mother's in bed and Dad's at pit. Russians break into Romania.

21st Mar

- Set some shallots but afterwards I pulled them up and set them properly. Bought Peg a birthday card. Hungary now cut off from rest of Europe.

22nd Mar

- Mr Fielding cleaned up for Mum when she was ill in bed. Wireless talk on post-war planes. It said some planes would be 3 times as big as our bombers. Bulgaria in midst of crashing.

23rd Mar

- Peggy Worsdale's birthday, age 22 years. Sent her a card. Nothing doing with toast fork. 1,000 ton raid on Frankfurt.

24th Mar

- Got pram off Dolly Spencer, baby is very well. Some peace coming up. Invasion soon, enemy will feel shock.

25th Mar

- Went to Don[caster] with Dad, put my new coat on for first time. 2,500 tons on Berlin.

26th Mar

- Baby one week old at ½ past 1 this morning. Russians sweeping towards Romania. Heard good joke today – Why has Hitler got straight hair? Because Britannia rules the waves.

27th Mar

- Football match between Skellow and Rossington. Rossington won 2-1. Koniev about to invade Romania.

28th Mar

- Went gardening on school gardens, spreading fertilizer and setting broad beans. Russian pressure grows on south.

29th Mar

- Wireless talk about why Hitler invaded Hungary. Wrote competition ad' out. Visit to parish church. Bombing still going on in Germany.

30th Mar

- Rossington miners strikes, 60,000 men striking all together. Went gardening down behind [bouser??]. Confidence debate begins.

31st Mar

- Still on strike. No news from Italy. Nuremburg bombed. RAF's biggest loss of 96 bombers.

1st Apr

- Agnes Worsdale got married. Peg sent us a parcel with oranges and chocolate.

2nd Apr

- Forgot to put clock back so late for church! New Russian offensive.

3rd Apr

- No wireless talks. 6 Germans shoot 41 airmen. Started salute the soldier poster at school. Found a pencil sharpener.

4th Apr

- Swift changing moves by Russians. Gardening man came to school to start farmers club for boys who keep livestock. Peace coming up. Budapest blitzed again.

5th Apr

- Rossington lost football at Armthorpe 3-1. Got top shield yesterday, 100%. Bevin acts cool in crisis. HOLIDAY TIL 17TH.

6th Apr

- Keith Sanderson left school today! The blue house won cup and shield. 60% of Yorkshire at work.

7th Apr

- Stood in a long queue for fish but got none. Terpitz, a big German war ship is sunk.

8th Apr

- Went to new baths for first time and had a good time. Russian ring closes around Odessa.

9th Apr

- No Easter eggs, it is not a bit like Easter. Russians at Czech frontier.

10th Apr

- Mother was churched today. Bill went to baths for first time. Germans abandon Odessa. Red army now in Czechoslovakia.

11th Apr

- Odessa falls to Russians. Another big Soviet push. I wish I was at school, nothing to do! Fighting still going slowly in Italy (Cassino).

12th Apr
- Set some more seeds. Fastest plane is Spitfire, next it is Thunderbolt 4041 and fastest bomber is Mosquito 380. Round the clock air offensive continues.

13th Apr
- Calours flit into Mumby's old shop. Lord Lonsdale dies at 27, great sportsman. Complete blockade clams Crimea.

14th Apr
- Ward sent one dozen eggs, some velveta cheese, and bought mum a Guiness. Crimean Dunkirk begins for Nazis.

15th Apr
- General Vatutin dies - Great Russian leader aged 44. Dad set spuds and joined gardening club. Went on a walk.

16th Apr
- Baby is 4 weeks old and cries alot. Constantinople falls, garrison wiped out.

17th Apr
- Holidays finish and exams begin. Nearly finished my Saluted the Soldier poster. Revision at school. Fall of Sevastopol very near, expected to fall tomorrow.

18th Apr
- Got to know about tech. They have not passed anyone in Rossington, only 15 places for 400 people. Sevastopol fighting for time.

19th Apr
- Navy crew have a special apparatus, they swim with it to big ships and fasten it on, they must be killed or prisoned. Navy secret our human torpedo.

20th Apr
- Rossington juniors beat Carcroft 4-0. Not done toast fork yet. Asked Mrs Fawcett for Bill Bakers reference. 9,000 tons in 36 hours. 6,000 planes.

21st Apr
- Got 2 birds eggs. Venice bombed by allies. R.A.F. pound west front railway. 1,100 heavies hit four centres.

22nd Apr

- Found hedge sparrows egg. Mosquitos bomb Germans with 4,000 tons. Biggest air armada yet. 80,000 boats ready for invasion.

23rd Apr

- Day of prayer. Baby 5 weeks old. Results, woodwork 76, metalwork 78, English 62, poetry 26, reading 29, science 86.

24th Apr

- Raymond started school and went without crying, just sat in his place as calm as anything. Big Air Armada over Germany.

25th Apr

- Set potatoes all afternoon. At school got wood pigeons egg, French blackie, and song thrush. Pay as you earn going well says Sir John.

26th Apr

- Gordon Fielding's birthday age 9.Wireless talk on Crimea. Sebastopol has been sieged 8 times as allied invasion comes nearer. Wave of sabotage rises.

27th Apr

- Went bird nesting today and got chased. A few bombs in Doncaster on football pitch. Great R.A.F raid on Essen (Krupps).

28th Apr

- Mr Robson one of our teachers leaves school. Came second in science with 86, Bill came third with 85.

29th Apr

- Sudden death of Colonel Knox aged 70. Many bombers bomb Oslo and great damage done. Bill invited to Fielding's party. Climax is near says Berlin.

30th Apr

- Greatest air battle in history. Found blacky's nest with 4 in. Got pint of milk for 2d.

1st May

- New rocket guns. Found a lot of strips of paper, Germans drop it to stop radio. Finished poster. Day and night pounding of French targets.

2nd May

- Made garden in front of Mr Fawcet's Lobby tidy. Steel house built in three days. Empire Premiers hear plans for invasion.

3rd May

- Wireless talk on the water supply, how the army is supplied. Talk on the future of houses.

4th May

- Enemy speculate on airborn landing. Doctor at school this morning giving lecture on sleep and food. Film show at school. Big air raid on France.

5th May

- Rained all day! Six spuds up, row of radish knocked down. Finished all exams. Pas-de-Calais bombed today.

6th May

- Aunt came down and baked a lot of cakes. Big new exploit by RAF. Dam burst threat to Germany.

7th May

- Baby christened today. All is ready for final phase of air onslaught.

8th May

- Science 86 History 86. Had first cricket house match. Had good party yesterday (Bill Burton, Gordon Spen)

9th May

- Went bird nesting and found nest with five in, think it was a Yellow Hammer's. 2000 planes bomb Berlin.

10th May

- Wireless talk about occupied countries, 3 children were the speakers. Sevastopol falls after 3 weeks.

11th May

- Got my toast fork done! Came 7th in exams at school, 2nd in science. Allies to plan New League talks on world security soon. I got a bike.

12th May

- July 10th 1943 landing in Sicily, September 3rd landing on mainland, September 8th Italy surrenders, September 9th landing at Salerno, October 1st Naples occupied, March 15th (44) allies thrusts into Cassino.

13th May

- Set some peas and potatoes. Fifth and eighth take several heights near Gustav. Bridgehead established over rapids.

14th May

- Outer ring of Gustav line shattered.

15th May

- Changed Bob blue tits for brown finches. Gustav line breached by allies. French capture Ausonia.

16th May

- The war is costing £13¼ million a day. 3000 German prisoners from Gustav. Allies keep up big drive in Italy line. Eighth army punching in Loire valley.

17th May

- Wireless talk about Mr Curtis, a gunsmith. Eighth army pressing Hun rear line.

18th May

- Got 16 eggs now, got Jays today. Germans shoot 47 reinforcement officers trying to escape from Stalag luft

19th May

- Had 1 days metalwork and half days woodwork. Fifth widen west flank. Nearly finished toast fork.

20th May

- Salute the soldier starts today. Rosso's target £25,000, schools £400. Hitler line is breached. Allies chase Hun back to last ditch, switch position.

21st May

- Link up drive 35 miles from Anzio's. Went in church parade to the chapel.

22nd May
- Played in house match. Rita Kegg's birthday age 12. £75 by end of day saved by school. Fifth swoop on to take Fordi

23rd May
- By end of day school saved £260, target £300. York and Lancs band on market. Fifth take switch line hills.

24th May
- Had concert at school and empire wireless talk. Royal Army Veterinary Corps gave exhibition today. Allies piece Anzio perimeter.

25th May
- All peas, spuds, shallots and all other things are growing good. Link up with bridgehead (Anzio) today. Terracina falls, Hitler line smashed.

26th May
- School beats its target of £300 by £180. Broke up. Allies now 21 miles from Rome.

27th May
- Got Cuckoos egg today, it was in hedge sparrows which had 4 in. Allies now only 18 miles from Rome. Fifth army has nearly closed trap on Germany.

28th May
- Doncaster rural district beats target (£125,000) with total up to 5 o' Clock today £180,140. Allies have 25,000 trapped.

29th May
- Went to Wheatley Hills boating lake, a long queue. Fifth army only 16½ miles from Rome. British capture Aprilia (prisoners total 15,000).

30th May
- Fifth pounding city's last line. Eighth army rolling up highway six. Went bathing down Waddy (Wadworth). Eighth fighting hard all the way.

31st May
- Allies now only 15 miles from Rome. British dent Rome line flank. Went to Donny, Keith treated me to the pictures and to dinner in the corn exchange.

1st June

- Went to see concert called 'Quaker Girl'. Allies penetrate the Rome line while eight closes in. Highway 6 cut at Valmontane.

2nd June

- Germans facing new crisis. RAF strike again at French rails. Fifth army gain foothold on Alban hills. U.S. troops see Rome. Russians to strike on 15th.

3rd June

- Wondering when invasion will start. Set some cabbage plants. Germans report allied advance to within 12 miles of Rome. Allies will spare Rome if possible.

4th June

- Gen Wilson came in for dinner at 4 O'clock. Allies break through Alban Hills. Fifth and eighth link up on highway 6. Ridge cleared. Downhill drive for Rome is near.

5th June

- Rosso total for salute the soldier was £26,000, target was £20,000. Fifth army liberate Rome. Germans pursued across Tiber. Sarson had nightingales egg at school.

6th June

- Normandy invasion on north of France, invasion opened today just after dawn, 4,000 ships, 11,000 planes, and thousands of landing craft.

7th June

- Allies strengthen grip on Normandy 12½ miles inland in some places. 2,000 tons of shells in 10 minutes. Had Red Cross collection in pictures.

8th June

- Invasion troops capture Bayeux. Found Water Hen's with 5 (eggs) in. Had gardening instead of metal work.

9th June

- Brought toasting fork home. Tollo falls to allies in Italy. Allies build up the beachheads without half. Got some dates from Ward's.

10th June
- U.S. take important town in Normandy.

11th June
- We drive on along all fronts. Monty's headquarters now in assault area. Normandy flooded our gerry's.

12th June
- Capetown taken by allies. U.S. develop threat to Cherbourg. Was picked in six to throw cricket ball.

13th June
- Cherbourg hold firm at Laen. Montebourg falls today.

14th June
- Monty strikes at flank. In Normandy, bomber command dropped 400,000 tons since war began, 275,000 on Germany.

15th June
- Advance in peninsula, Caen wedge holds. Started coal rake at school.

16th June
- Cherbourg threat grows as allies build up. Going for another scholarship tomorrow, won a shilling for my poster at school.

17th June
- Germans sent bombers over controlled by radio. Cherbourg gains hold, Germans fail in Caen push.

18th June
- Germans sending plane over every 3 minutes. RAF blast secret works. Allies tighten Cherbourg noose. Strong front expert in school.

19th June
- Allies captured Elba yesterday. Cherbourg noose now secure. Lord Hay died today.

20th June
- 2nd week of invasion. Americans within 5 miles of Cherbourg. Came second in throwing cricket ball.

21st June
- Allies within 3 miles of sea. Allies ask Gerry's to surrender Cherbourg. Icon cricketer killed (Dodds). Big battle on sea with Jap's.

22nd June

- Nazi retreat in Italy continues. Fight for Cherbourg begins, 1000 bombers blast the town. Bob Wiles passes grammar school.

23rd June

- Cherbourg onslaught – progress satisfactory. Nearing climax. Got some tomatoes from Ward's. Keith said war would end October 11th – 13th.

24th June

- Americans 2000 yds from Cherbourg. Navy shell Cherbourg.

25th June

- Vital Cherbourg heights captured. Navy shatters evacuation attempt. Gerry's still sending flying bombs over. 8000 Jap's dead after latest attack.

26th June

- Peninsula port lost since 8 o'clock this morning, say Berlin. Hand fighting still going on in Cherbourg. Got two marrows this morning.

27th June

- Cherbourg fell this morning! British army casualties were 73,122 from Italy to fall of Rome. Killed 7635, wounded 23283, missing 5708.

28th June

- Montgomery's advance on 4 mile front in Normandy. A firm bridgehead over river. Wireless talk on the wounded.

29th June

- Padre and wounded shot by Gerry soldier, he crept in to the hostel and shot them. 2nd army tanks widen corridor near Caen.

30th June

- Big German counter attacks smashed near Caen. Minsk will very likely fall within 48 hours, says paper.

1st July

- Building up the [Saliatort??] west of Caen. Fall of Minsk in next few hours.

2nd July

- Fiercest Nazi blow in Caen. Area driven back.

3rd July

- Americans attack south from Cherbourg. Sienna, an Italian town falls to allies. Fine progress in Italy.

4th July

- Canadians take airfield village of Carpiquet 3 miles from Caen. Minsk falls to Russians. Battle for Poland has begun.

5th July

- Russians pace in record offensive to Vilna, Dvinsk, and Grodne. Germans say Montgomery is attacking Carentan. Cousin Ernie has been to see us.

6th July

- One killed by every flying bomb. (2,752 fatal casualties – 2,754 bombs). Russians drive on at 24 miles per day. Hitler orders use all reserves.

7th July

- Premier makes statement on flying bombs yesterday. Montgomery makes triple push in Normandy. British advance a mile near Caen.

8th July

- Saint Jean-de-Daye is captured. 2,300 tons of bombs on Caen. Great Russian drive west. Germans evacuate Vilna.

9th July

- Russians right in streets of Vilna. Aunt Martha's birthday. Evacuees came into Rosso yesterday. Monty's troops in Caen suburbs.

10th July

- Carentan taken by the allies say Germans. U.S. develops threat to Cherbourg from the neck. Picked in six to throw cricket ball.

11th July
- Allies hit out afresh today in Normandy. Went to Aunts silver wedding. Russians into Latvia Lithuania. Record speed of great Russian push. Went to Donny.

12th July
- British crush all counter blows on Arne line. Rommel is short of reserves. Russians still going well. No flying bombs on London.

13th July
- About forty evacuees came into Rossington about 6 o'clock. Baltic Panzer line ceases to exist. Only 35 miles to Germany.

14th July
- Nazis lose 500,000 in the Russians new offensive. Russians outflank Grodno today on a march for east Russia. 50 mile front opens on Niemen line, Minsk falls.

15th July
- Lord Summers – Chief Scout died yesterday. Red army's big guns punch at Grodno. Went to Waddy village, seen wrestling and boxing.

16th July
- Arretso falls to allies in Italy. Flying bombs over England. Grodno falls to Russians.

17th July
- Caen and La Haye in allied hands. Siapan falls (pacific island). Lida, an important town falls. Rommel now fighting in earnest. British hold firm on Orne Line Hills. 5 evacuees came into our class.

18th July
- Americans capture St Lo. 31 English prisoners shot by Romans. Red army enters Latvia. Went to baths at 5 o'clock.

19th July
- Acora falls to the Polish troops of the eigth army. Americans capture Leghorn.

20th July

- Russians 8 miles from East Prussia. Monty widens Orne line gap. All goes extremely well. 170,000 official evacuees from London.

21st July

- Hitler reveals plot to kill him "Criminal Clique". Put bomb at headquarters (6 yds away). Had concert at school, viola, clarinet, violin, cello.

22nd July

- Signs persist of anti Nazi revolt in Germany. Nothing from Normandy.

23rd July

- Russians outflank Kvov. New ration books start today.

24th July

- Hitlers Reich shows signs of weakness. Brought reports home from school. Mr Churchill says "Great turmoil in Germany". Russians speed up great advance.

25th July

- Lubin falls to great Russian drive. New drive starts in Normandy at 3:30 this morning.

26th July

- Russians 70 miles from Warsaw. Went to baths and learned to swim about 3 yards. Mr Rider one of our teachers has got 12 months in prison for hitting a lad.

27th July

- Deblin falls to Russians. Visula fortress falls. British fall back in Caen sector. Russians 45 miles from Warsaw.

28th July

- Went up into form 4 from 3a yesterday. Russians move to final stage of fight for Warsaw. Our subs sink 21 Jap ships. Broke window with golf ball. Broke up from School. Bob and Arch left school yesterday.

29th July

- Decisive battles for Warsaw and Cracow. Allies take Coutances and push south. Gypsy said war will end Aug 13th.

30th July

- Big retreat coming in south. Nazis 8th army can see Florence, Italy.

31st July

- Small advances in Caen sector. Went to see Snow White at Gaumont, stood from 1:15 to 2:30.

1st Aug
- Americans into Brittany. Got some apples from old village 8d per Lb.

2nd Aug
- Russians 12 miles from Prussia.

3rd Aug
- Ring of steel hems Villiers (Caen). Germans admit crisis on Normandy west flank. Flying bombs hit hospitals last night.

4th Aug
- Alan Burton home on leave from merchant navy.

5th Aug
- 142 days to Christmas.

6th Aug
- Brittany cut off. Allies into Brest.

7th Aug
- Capture of Fort Pinco, key to the south flanks. Lorient falls to Americans. British in drive across arne.

8th Aug
- 165 Gerry tanks Kroked out by RAF. Great new allied push in France after blitz. 6,000 tons of bombs in 10 minutes.

9th Aug
- 3,000 Japs killed in battle for Myitkyina. Americans take Hep??? in sweep towards Paris.

10th Aug
- Americans enter Nantes. New drive from Orne bridgehead. Warsaw showdown. A proactive new British push.

11th Aug
- Breaking Orne front, river now crossed in three places. Allies 41 miles from Paris.

12th Aug
- Big Sheffield fire £100,000 worth of damage to Fargate store yesterday. British slashing into Bulge.

13th Aug

- Went to baths. Plenty of apples out now. Great allied trap closing escape gap. Reduced to 35 miles from Normandy. Florence liberated. 300,000 fell yesterday. Burtons got a baby today.

14th Aug

- Germans in full retreat towards Seine line. Flying bombs damage 7000 houses an hour.

15th Aug

- New allied landing near France. Marseille 800 tons, ships, and thousands of airborne troops.

16th Aug

- Went to baths. Allied go ahead in south France as planned. Vast air umbrella. Riviera invasion supplies pour in. Allied troops fighting in Falaise.

17th Aug

- Falaise escape gap only 6 miles wide. Allies sent from Paris. Orleans falls. Went to Hexthorpe, had a good day. Germans in northern France.

18th Aug

- Battle for Normandy is won 20 miles from Paris. RAF destroys 150 German tanks.

19th Aug

- Pilots fly 6 hours to Warsaw to Polish patriots who are fighting there. Sir Henry Wood dies.

20th Aug

- French patriots occupy Vichy.

21st Aug

- Aunt Beck's birthday. Patton's forces at gates of Paris. U.S. troops pouring across Seine. Progress in southern France.

22nd Aug

- Threat to Marseilles. Princess Margaret Rose's birthday yesterday age 14. 30,000 Germans captured in Calais pockets.

23rd Aug

- Paris liberated by French patriots. 50,000 patriots rise inside Paris. Had quarter of an hour's extra play. (Bill's first metalwork lesson).

24th Aug

- Romania comes onto our side. No sign of stand on Seine. Marseilles falls. Had 10 minutes extra play.

25th Aug

- Billy Worsdales birthday, age 12 years. Got no parcels! Drive to Danube and Calais. Hitler orders all Cinamers etc to be closed down owing to lack of manpower.

26th Aug

- Allies enter liberated Paris.

27th Aug

- France retreats to Siegfried line. 130 miles to Germany. Bulgaria seeking peace.

28th Aug

- Louise Gray, Don Winner from pin-up comp. Marne line reported abandoned by Germans. Fall of Calais opens Balkans to Russia. No flying bombs over London for 77 hours.

29th Aug

- Russians striking for Brasov, vital Hungary junction.

30th Aug

- Russians 17 miles from Bucharest. Every foot gained at Caen was as much as 10 anywhere else, says Monty.

31st Aug

- Russians enter Bucharest. Monty made a field Marshall today.

1st Sep

- Dieppe Falls. Verdun falls and opens road to Germany. Monty's men take Nazi 14th army commander. Calais entered.

2nd Sep

- British take Vimy ridge in great sweep. Allies 50 miles from Germany. Allies advanced 4 miles in 24 hours.

3rd Sep

- War's 5 year ends. American spearheads in Belgium. Finnish orders cease fire.

4th Sep

- BRUSSELS FALLS to British 2nd Army. 300 mile of Siegfried Line directly threatened. British 2nd Army covers 130 miles in four and a half days. Tanks covered with flowers. British 25 miles from Dutch border.

5th Sep

- Lyons falls, Antwerp falls. British 12 miles over Dutch border. Bulgaria and Hungary entered. Bourg falls.

6th Sep

- Went to film show. VON KLUGE dead. Died from heart attack 12 days ago. Allies enter Luxembourg. British in Holland. Allies isolate Calais in channel ports drive.

7th Sep

- BLACKOUT WILL BE LIFTED on Sunday 17th! No compulsory Home Guard parades now. No fire practice (my dad used to practice putting out

a fire in our upstairs bedroom with a hose pipe fitted into the notch at the end of our clothes prop - while I pumped). Advance continues.

8th Sep

- British 2nd Army breaks across Albert (?) canal. Balkan trap for 200,000 Nazis - all out offensive cuts escape gaps.

9th Sep
- Bulgaria declares war on Germany. German Army remnant doomed at Dunkirk (?).

10th Sep
- British smash counter attacks. British make bridge over Albert Canal. No more flying bombs now.

11th Sep
- British strengthen bridgehead over Albert Canal. Forces in north and south of France join up.

12th Sep
- Allies enter Germany. 10 miles over Reich frontier at one or two points. Nazis surrender at Havre after 36 hours of all-out attacks.

13th Sep
- 6 western Armies, led by Greece, blitz Germany. German frontier crossed again, 60 miles from last crossing. Sister Peggy came home on leave from Waffs (RAF).

14th Sep
- Allies press westward and beat counter attacks. Canadians cross Leopold Canal. Gerrys lose 37 fighter planes in 3 days. Russians in Warsaw suburbs.

15th Sep
- Siegfried Line in contact with Warsaw in Russian hands (?). Empire blow against Japs soon.

16th Sep
- Main Siegfried line is broken, tanks roll through. Eisenhower hitting out on 500 mile front (Tehran wins St. Ledger).

17th Sep
- Blackout lifted. Tonight was the first time my brother Ray (born 21/11/1939) saw the lights. Sky troops land in Holland.

18th Sep
- New air landings in Holland.

19th Sep

- Charles is 6 months old today. War in Europe will be over this year.

20th Sep

- British race for the Rhine, 50 mile advance. More supplies flown to Holland. Boulogne falls.

21st Sep

- British forces capture Rhine Bridge intact. Armour across. 40,000 prisoners at Brest.

22nd Sep

- Dempsey's tanks near Arnhem Airborne troops reached. Soldiers will get extra pay after 3 years and Far East extra.

23rd Sep

- Waal crossed, way shown by young boy. Dempsey reaches river top at Arnhem.

24th Sep

- Caruso shot today, secretary gets 30 years.

25th Sep

- British now have armour corridor to Lek river line. Germans weakening s of Arnhem. (Today will be the last day of siege of British troops at Arnhem.

26th Sep

- Bad weather stops bombing on Germans. Position at Arnhem unchanged.

27th Sep

- Arnhem came back through enemy line. Blankets round boots, most had had no sleep for 6 days.

28th Sep

- Mr Churchill says that Arnhem battle was the most daring battle of war. British corridor widened in Holland. Only 2000 came back out of 8000.

29th Sep

- Hitler's hopes of retaking Nijmegen Bridge fade away. British building up for new drive over Rhine.

30th Sep
- Nijmegen Bridge secure in British hands. Enemy positions shift every week. Slanging match along Dutch front.

St Luke's Church - Rossington

1st Oct

- Mr Worsdales birthday age 44.

2nd Oct

- Went potato picking. New allied drive for Siegfried.

3rd Oct

- U.S. troops reported half through Siegfried line. Calais falls to Canadians. RAF bomb Dutch canals.

4th Oct

- Dunkirk has Calais truce. 60 hours to remove civilians. 20,000 will be evacuated from Dunkirk. 2m line torn in Siegfried.

5th Oct

- New landing in Greece, Pathos falls. Fighting every 5 yards now.

6th Oct

- Rion falls (Greece). Allies advance towards Greek capital (Athens). New Canadian assault on Shelt Pocket. Hun plight worsens. Last storming of Dunkirk has begun.

7th Oct

- Allies continue advance into Holland. Firm bridgehead across Leopold canal. Talk of new air landings. Patriots and Germans fight in Greek capital. Repatriated men at front again. Hun breaches laws of the war.

8th Oct

- 30,000 tons and 7,500 planes in biggest ever blitz on Germany! Americans break through north of Aachen. Spearhead thrusts 4m into Germany.

9th Oct

- Mr Churchill and Mr Eden fly to Moscow. Great new battle in E. Prussia. Silent flying bomb. Latest Nazi threat! Nazis new K-boats. Supposed to travel faster than sound and can raid America. Canadians land in Scaeld estuary today.

10th Oct

- Had letter from Peg. Nazi internal mystery on Moscow talk. £5 each has been given to (one hdo?) bombed out people from Croydon. Rumour that Goering has been arrested.

11th Oct
- Aachen told, give in or be destroyed. Guns and planes ready to blow it off the map.

12th Oct
- Frank Worsdales birthday, age 14 yrs. Peg sent me a diary. Americans keep up heavy pounding of Aachen.

13th Oct
- Athens falls to Greek patriots. Risa falls to Russians. *LEFT SCHOOL*.

14th Oct
- Germans loose 84 tons in Arnhem fighting. Churchill fly's to Moscow.

15th Oct
- Rommel, one of Germans best generals, dies. Hungary wants armistice.

16th Oct
- Himmler reported in Budapest to keep Hungary in the war. Germans control capital. Admiral Horty takes refuge in ancient castle.

17th Oct
- BLANK

18th Oct
- Athens falls to Partisans. Tidim falls to Indian troops in Burma.

19th Oct
- Allies strike afresh in Aachen. Philippines invaded (Leyte).

20th Oct
- Belgrade falls. Aachen falls. Moscow conference ends.

21st Oct
- Allies 100 miles past Athens. Moscow conference ends, great results.

22nd Oct
- War over by winter (Moscow talks).

23rd Oct
- BLANK

24th Oct
- Swift E. Prussian campaign planned. Immediate threat to Insterburg. Red army moves on broad plain 50 miles from Konigsberg.

25th Oct

- Japanese fleet at last forced to action in Pacific. Wars biggest air sea battle in Philippines, enemy carrier sunk. British cut life lines in west Holland.

26th Oct

- Roosevelt announces decisive defeat of Jap fleet. Every ship either sunk or damaged. British gain 8 miles in drive for Tilburg.

27th Oct

- BLANK

28th Oct

- 40,000 Germans threatened in Holland.

29th Oct

- 40,000 Germans on the run.

30th Oct

- British driving Germans towards Maas Bridges. 3 Miles from river at one point. Schelt nearly free of enemy.

31st Oct

- Churchill says war may go on until summer 1945. Election unlikely for 7 or 9 months. Allies win battles of W. Holland.

1st Nov

- Allies push all but Hun rear guards across Maas. British front 1000 yds from Maas. Artillery threatens the bridges.

2nd Nov

- Started work as apprentice painter. German commander and 2500 men taken in Schell.

3rd Nov

- Americans shoot down 280 enemy planes in Cologne raid. Russians gain great Budapest, flushing fails.

4th Nov

- Hungarian capitals capture is imminent. Now only 3 miles away.

5th Nov

- Battling to German gateway, Antwerp open soon. Big allied action coming soon, says Nazis.

6th Nov

- More allied advances to river. Excellent progress made in West Holland, S.H.E.A.F. Germans goodbye to Waicheren

7th Nov

- Thursday 2nd, started work as apprentice painter and decorator with Mr Osborne, 4 St. Vincent Avenue, Doncaster.

8th Nov

- BLANK

9th Nov

- Patton widens Saar. Front push advances upto 3 miles.

10th Nov

- V2 is stratosphere rocket bomb. 60 to 70 mile outstrips sound. Some sites overrun. England under fire for last few weeks.

11th Nov

- Churchill and Eden in Paris on Armistice Day. France seeks partnership.

12th Nov

- France, the big three Premier invites Degeville to enter Europe.

13th Nov

- Stalin asks Mr Churchill and Mr Roosevelt to confer. Big three invitation to Moscow reported. Paton still near. Tirpitz sunk.

14th Nov

- Tirpitz sunk by 29 Lancaster's carrying 12,000 Lb bombs (Earthquake bomb)!

15th Nov

- Hitler three direct hits. Dempsey forces Germans to withdraw from Dutch canal line. British take all first objectives near Maas. 3 British heads now joined.

16th Nov

- Hitler mystery deepens.

17th Nov

- Six army's open winter offensive. 1st and 9th launch new drive into Rhinesland. Dempsey's troops nearing gateway to Ruhr.

18th Nov

- British cross Zig canal to nip out last Maas pocket. Hodges' Aachen push now 25 miles from Rhine. Dempsey's progress is good. Miss Jean Kent at Gaumont today.

19th Nov

- Charles is 8 months old today.

20th Nov

- Robert Pines birthday, 3. Had day off work, had haircut.

21st Nov

- Raymond Worsdale's birthday age 5. Germans retreat on 100 mile front. In the west fighting reported in Saarebourg. Tanks near Rhine at Mulhouse.

22nd Nov

- Peg sent Ray a pencil case. Allies press steadily towards the Ruhr. Big fights yet to come in west.

23rd Nov

- British 2nd Army fights strong towards Rhine. Allies on 2 lines that guard the Ruhr. Dempsey at Maas on 16 mile front.

24th Nov
- Pay day £1-2s-4d for 6 days. Left my job. Tokyo bombed by super forts from new bases on Leyte.

25th Nov
- Biggest German line up singe Normandy. Monty gets chance he has been waiting for. Tokyo left ablaze.

26th Nov
- Germans say they are facing heavies. Allies smash into Cologne plain.

27th Nov
- British casualties to September 1944 have been 6,600,000 killed, wounded, or prisoner. 134,000 civilians killed or injured.

28th Nov
- 5,500,000 in armed forces since war. Britain has produced 102,000 aeroplanes, 25,000 tanks, 35,000 guns, 5,700 ships, and saved upwards of 48,000,000,000

29th Nov
- Victory session of parliament opened. The King voices the nations mind, he spoke for 13 minutes. Many measures for post war period.

30th Nov
- Peg goes to Newcastle for her leave.

1st Dec

- 9th Army has nearly won battle of west Roer. Last towns being cleared.

2nd Dec

- Penge, one of the worst blitzed boroughs of London has been adopted by Doncaster.

3rd Dec

- Rossington Home Guard finished today, they kept their uniform.

4th Dec

- E.L.A.S. take some police station in Athens.

5th Dec

- Greece faced with desperate economic and financial problems trying to stop civil war in Greece.

6th Dec

- British tanks open fire in Athens. Troops police Athens to prevent civil war. Ravena captured by Lances.

7th Dec

- E.L.A.S. holds nearly all police stations in Athens. Greeks must decide for themselves says Churchill.

8th Dec

- 7,000 E.L.A.S. gathering outside Athens.

9th Dec

- Bob sent me a book for Xmas, 'Young Fur Traders'.

10th Dec

- Peace move hopes in Holland. Nazis lose 158,000 men in 22 days.

11th Dec

- Great eastern gateway to Germany within Russian grasp. Germans are today abandoning Budapest.

12th Dec

- Charles got 2 more teeth. Situation still uneasy in Athens. Big three talks in Jan.

13th Dec

- Got ½lb of nuts off cunar, first since war (Almond, Hazel nuts). Bill brings his first model home (Spitfire). Rays school party.

14th Dec
- Major Munson awarded B.E.M. Major of Ross Home Guard.

15th Dec
- Got ½lb of nuts off Ward and jar of mincemeat (1lb).

16th Dec
- Sent Bob Harris a tie for Xmas. British army competent to deal with rebels. Gen Platras. Regency council for Greece near at hand.

17th Dec
- Premier reported in favour of big three talk.

18th Dec
- Dad wrote letter to Aunt Edna (Armitage). Ray brought Xmas card home. Germans launch big attack. Still gaining ground in all out west attack. Allies have counter measured.

19th Dec
- Charles 9 months old.

20th Dec
- Germans 20 miles into Belgium.

21st Dec
- Rundstedt still pushing on. He may have struck too soon.

22nd Dec
- Nazis 35 miles into Belgium.

23rd Dec
- Deepest Nazi thrust 35 miles into Belgium. 30 miles from Sedan.

24th Dec
- Rundstedt held in north, drives on in south. Some flying bombs came over Rossington last night. One fell in Rosso near Hall.

25th Dec
- Charles first Christmas. Peg sent me a dictionary. Dad and Mam gave me 2/6 and a set of draughts.

26th Dec
- Coldest Xmas since 1890. No snow but very frosty.

27th Dec
- Tony John age 15 (27.12.29) No.2 Firth Crescent, Rossington.

28th Dec

- Snow bound in Italy. Jap losses 116,000, Leyte island, Sun 31st.

29th Dec

Britain gets biggest earthquake for years, we felt it, it was only in north.

30th Dec

- Greek Archbishop approved Regent. Halted nearly all parts of fronts.

31st Dec

- Germans face final showdown. Russian white flag men shot by Nazis (Budapest).

Post script.

- Sicily falls, August 1943.
- Looked at mason marks in old Rossington.
- Mainland invaded 3rd Sept 1943
- Italy's unconditional surrender 9th Sept 1943.
- The mill keeps on rolling.
- Tony Johnson left school 22nd Dec 1943
- Got some tools for Xmas off Mam and Dad, 2/6 off peg.
- ? off Aunty Edner
- Jigsaw off Aunt Becca, Black Swan 6/- off Shaws at Pictures.
- Mussolini overthrown 8th Sept 1943
- Went potato picking Oct 8th to Nov 1st, earned £4/15s/-
- Baby's weight last week (Tuesday 5th) 11lb 7oz, 6 months old.
- Argentina breaks relations with Germany, Sunday 30th Jan 1944.
- Flitted 6th February 1944 because next door kept knocking on wall and wakening dad up.
- Up to Jan 1944, Malta has had 2,000 air raids.
- 200,000 B.C. Axe head found at Mount Pleasant, Rossington – 28th Feb 1944.

1946

1st Jan

- No one let New Year in. Tony the milk man was first to burst in at 8:30am this morning. A nice nippy morning. Rail disaster dead rises to 13.

2nd Jan

- Two families nearly wiped out in Lichfield train disaster. The L.M.S. disaster at Lichfield (Staffs) station on Trent Valley main line death role rises to 17, only 6 of 40 passengers escape unhurt. "Slaughter all British Commando's", Hitler ordered in 1942. The trial of leading Nazi war criminals continues today. 550lb German bomb found at Eastbourne, it will be exploded tomorrow.

3rd Jan

- William Joyce (Lord Haw-Haw of the German radio) was hanged a 9 o'clock this morning. Went to concert at Welfare Hall 1/-, had 4/9 tips. Eastbourne bomb was safely exploded this morning.

4th Jan

- Reich Generals craved Nazi success until they saw methods. German staff climbed onto Hitler's bandwagon, too dangerous then to object. Britain in clear by 1950 says Morrison (economic difficulties). Lichfield trains dead rises to 19, three died in hospital. It was freezing yesterday, milder today but water was still turned to ice. Peg coming on leave on Monday 8th. (2s. 2d. tips)

5th Jan

- Ten killed and many injured in L.N.E.R. train crash near Durham, (London to Edinburgh) early this morning. 1/4 tips. We had an extra ¼lb of sweets for xmas they go back to the old ration of 12oz on Sunday! The magna Carta which has been in safe keeping in Washington since 1939 world fair will start its journey back to Britain on the 11th Jan. New army de-mob list will keep to 58,000 out per week. Air ministry says cold snap is over, gales next.

6th Jan

- Started building prefabs behind the New Hotel half way through the permanent houses in Rosso stockyard. Science finishes as not enough attended.

7th Jan

- Missing

8th Jan

- Missing

9th Jan

- Missing

10th Jan

- Norman Baillie Stewart gets 5 years penal servitude; he is not British at heart and may return to Germany. The U.N.O. assembly begins peace drive this afternoon at 4:15pm (51 nations taking part). The Prime Minister (Attlee) calls on 51 nations to shape new world. The atom problem will be dealt with in the U.N.O. assembly. 540 are killed on the roads every month. Bill went to join St. Luke's church choir tonight. Had John Bull paper, first this morning. Conisborough Urban Council have bought from Lord Yarborough Conisborough Castle for £25 (plus 5.6 acres).

11th Jan

- The second day of U.N.O. was opened by the newly elected president of U.N.O. Mr. Spaak the Belgium foreign minister by a speech. Mr. Morrison has ended his tour of Canada and is on his way to New York. Mr. Roosevelt looks around London today. (Dad off work). Amateur radio to start soon. China now entering smooth waters after 15 years of intermittent civil war. The world is united as never before (Attlee)

12th Jan

- Peg goes back to camp, gave me, Bill, Ray, and Charlie 2s each. (U.N.O.) Nations that joins Security Council figures in brackets denote votes cast: Brazil (47), Egypt (45), Mexico (45), Poland (39), and Nederland (3?)

13th Jan

- Mr(s)? Green applied for me 10 extra clothing coupons, (for shop smocks). Russian delegate (U.N.O.) fails to win security election, lost vote 9 to 34. Worked at Green's for 12 months on Feb 14th (paid every Saturday £1). Club had £4 - 17s - 4½d in. Frosty weather expected soon.

14th Jan

- Bevin tells U.N.O. "stop lobbying". Morrison tells USA what we suffered during the war. Went to 9:30 communion and 6:30.

15th Jan

- The case begins against Admiral Karl Doenitz 55yr old engineer's son who rose to command the German Navy and ultimately became Feuhrer of Insburg when Reich collapsed (Nurremburg). Hitler ordered him to kill (torpedo) seamen and he obeyed. Industry facing black week. 280,000 phone workers postpone strike for a month. On Wednesday, ?000 meat workers will strike. Tomorrow ?000 United Electric Union workers go on strike. U.N.O. in London has completed the work of electing its main committee and cleared the way for its first big debate this evening. Mr Peter Fraser, Newzealand Prime Minister announced that his country would draw in favour of Yugoslavia for the social and economic council. £4 in Yorkshire Penny Bank, first time! Nothing to do at work (Green's) on Monday just stood about. Don't like it (no orders). Frosty this morning. Dad has a boil as big as a penny on his hand

16th Jan

- Half day. Wood and Metalwork at night school. Oranges came to Green's yesterday (1lb per book), Mrs. Green gave me 2 Jaffa's at dinnertime. Trailed around Doncaster for pair of long pants to match best coat, could not find any. Started hoe at night school.

17th & 18th Jan

- Missing

19th Jan

- 2,000,000 workers out in America. France wants Europe stronger in U.N.O. 15 states (150,000,000 people) are unrepresented says Mr. M. Georges Bidauld, French Foreign Minister. People in Leeds queue for over an hour for 9½d worth of coalite. Put in my order for bike front wheel. 38,000 hand-picked men (police) to police U.S. zone of Germany. Got some priority dockets for: 1 bed mattress, 2 blankets, 3 sheets, and ordered 3 months. Britain beats Belgium in football at Wembley 2.0

20th Jan

- Britain shivered yesterday as the icy spell went on unbroken all over the country and we shall be shivering again today. The outlook is cold, or very cold, with rain, sleet, or snow, and fog in many parts of the country. 92,000 stems' bananas (second lot) arrived at Liverpool yesterday. They will be divided among Liverpool, Manchester, and Belfast. First big job for Security Council as Persia takes plunge and appeals to U.N.O. The dispute is with Russia over Azerbaijan, soviet counter, Minority rights ignored. Went to Holy Communion at 9:30am, pumped (the organ) at 6:30pm, Mr. Roebuck away with flu.

21st Jan

- British Foreign secretary urges U.N.O. to get on with task. Bevin averts hold-up in atom inquiry, world upset if we delay. Frost made Big Ben grind at 9pm last night (ice in cogs). All England shivers in big freeze up. Coldest - North Midlands this winter. 23 days of frost on Sunday night. Green's gets some rope which is sold at 3/- per lb (25 yds). Snow still in Rosso. Biggest U.S. strike is over. 800,000 out in steel industry. Persian cabinet resigns, U.N.O. test may be averted.

22nd Jan

- Russia charges Britain: Raises Greece and Java issues, Molotov bombshell late last night. He asked if they should bring the Greece situation before the U.N.O. Uno can outlaw the A-Bomb says Truman. Mr Vyshinsky arrived in Britain at 12:58pm, set off from Berlin at 9:12am GMT. Warmer today, snow nearly all gone. Temperatures rising all over Britain. Doncaster's future school plan estimated cost

£968,000, 26 new buildings and 16 old ones to go. Half day, went metalwork at 4pm. Bill goes to choir practice. Bananas at Doxey's (Rosso).

23rd Jan

- U.N.O. puts off debate on Atom bomb. USA wants Persia and Greece discussed before Byrnes leaves. Speed up attempt failed, drastic strike move by USA state taking over meat packing industry. Election of French premier postponed. The zoning of Beer ends March 2nd. Snowed all day could not settle (only in dry parts). Went woodwork. Signed form for extra ten clothing coupons. Dad went to pit compo doctor to see if his hand was beet, he said no, two other doctors say yes. We will see in 2 weeks, he has to go to Sheffield referee.

24th Jan

- People's investments will be in grip of state, bill plans control of issues over £50,000. Mr. Felix Govin, France's new Premier says Spain is heading for democracy. Went pictures (in stalls). Mr Byrnes is ready to go to U.S. this afternoon or evening by plane. Ice this morning (thawed).

25th Jan

- Insurance scheme to cost £425,000,000, illness, unemployment, and old age. Benefits rose. Radar contact with the moon has been made by the U.S. army corps scientists, possibility of controlling rockets there, high frequency energy pulses were sent out and reflected back in about 2½ seconds (at speed of light). The Magna Carta was taken back to Lincoln Cathedral yesterday afternoon (from USA). Keith gave in notice at Jackson's garage Doncaster and Tony gives notice at Doxey's (milk), will take Co-op milk after. Britain loans Greece £10,000,000, the £46,000,000 Britain lent before has been turned into gift. No sign of snow today, quite warm (rain).

26th Jan

- Greece to tell U.N.O. "We want British to stay". A 4,500ft single span bridge is to be built over Humber from Hessle (Hull) on Yorkshire side and Barton on the Lincolnshire side; it will cost £6,400,000 (300ft longer than Golden Gate Bridge, California). 250,000 US meat strikers vote to stay on strike. More banana's in England. (Pay day £1). Bank of England £5 notes dated before Sept 2nd 1942 are to be called in on Feb 28th, 1946.

27th Jan

- RAF in some parts of India, they have a genuine grievance and are on strike. Slow rate of demoralisation at root of trouble. USA motor buses agree to give the strikers 18½ cents (11d) and hour and the strikers will soon be back at work (Ford and Chrysler motors). Frost and ice this morning, missed Communion 1st this year, went evensong 6:30pm.

28th Jan

- 4,000,000 soviet citizens were killed and tortured during the German occupation of the Ukraine. 20 G.I. (US) brides returned to England. America was not the dreamland they had thought it to be (went by air last summer). RAF men in biggest (India) strike yet. Made 10 day offer (6000) men. They are giving 10 days for governments to meet their demands (slow demob). Petition sent to Mr. Attlee. U.N.O. now discussing Russo-Persia disputes. Bill goes to choir practice at 6:30pm. Our Club (Mam, Dad, Bill, Ray, and Frank) has got £5-13s-0d in it. Dad draws £1-17s-6d out of Ray's school bank for sheets. Ray goes to Doncaster for eyes tested at Rayners and need to go again in 3 months. Dad still off work with bad hand. Very windy.

29th Jan

- Half day. Singapore paralysed by general strike, even essential services abandoned. More RAF men come out on strike. Noise waves from the sun, Australian scientists claim radar contact with sun for first time. Got 2 sheets from Doncaster. Bill off school with touch of flu. US atom bomb test on warships will cost £125,000,000 if not more according to US Navy figures.

30th Jan

- Mr. Trygve Lie has been appointed secretary general of U.N.O. (he is the Norwegian Foreign Minister). He is now the most powerful man in the world (Daily Express). British authorities have decided to permit 15,000 Jewish immigrants to enter Palestine per month. Singapore

RAF strike may be called off. Army taking over RAF jobs. Mr H. Hopkins died yesterday aged 56, he was President Roosevelt's closest adviser and confident.

31st Jan

- Sent away for book called 'The Self Educator' to the John Bull paper deluxe edition 6/3d. Mr Churchill and Lord Halifax have been put on the list of pallbearers for Mr. Harry Hopkins who died on Tuesday; the funeral takes place this afternoon in Nuremburg. A documented account of the massacre of 129 US soldiers, at Malmedy, France, during the retreat, German Ardennes offensive, in December 1944 was today presented to the international tribunal trying the 21 major Nazi's, Eternal shame of German Army.

1ST Feb

- Field Marshall Montgomery has been appointed chief of imperial general staff with effect on June 26th; he will succeed Field Marshall Allenbrook. Lady Astor arrives in USA. There will be no more dried eggs after tomorrow (Saturday), big rush all over Britain, Meadow, Rossington sells 900 packets. The clothing industry is now turning out 97,000 suits per week for demob soldiers, (if you order a suit now you have to wait 6 months). Last RAF strike in India is over. Figs come to Green's.

2nd Feb

- Bevan Vysinsky duel on Greece brings up wider issues, Anglo-Russian world relations at stake. Supreme test for U.N.O. on Monday. 4,500 cases of oranges arrive in Doncaster. Banana's expected next week (unripe). Strife grows in Greece. Right and left wing parties at odds. James Mason, Britain's number 1 film star will shortly go to Hollywood. Dad been off work for 3 weeks with bad hand.

3rd Feb

- World unity imperilled by Anglo-Soviet rift, U.N.O. behind scenes move t avert great crisis. Tomorrows fateful meeting of the Security Council has been preceded by a week of anxious discussions behind closed doors. A German bomb dropped in Hull 2½ years ago was removed yesterday from Hull Market place (2,500 lb). Went Communion at 9:30am and pumped church organ, also 6:30pm. Worked at Green's for 1 year on the 14th of this month.

4th Feb

- The U.N.O. Security Council are now dealing with the Greek issue, when the Security Council meet later today it will resume discussion of the Soviet complaint about the continued presence of British forces in Greece (floods of telegrams from rival parties in Greece). Conflicting Soviet demand. Oranges arrive in Rossington (1lb per head). Went to ENSA show at Welfare Hall (price 9d). Bill still off school (got a cold).

5th Feb
- Search is now going on for a formula for the Greek situation (U.N.O.) There are going to be 2 schools built in Rossington shortly (Infants and Boys Secondary). Sir Ben Smith, food minister, announced in the commons today that he had decided to reduce butter, margarine, and lard, from 8oz to 7oz per week by making the lard ration 1oz instead of 2oz per week. Bill attended choir practice tonight. Half day, did not go to Doncaster, went to metalwork at 7 o'clock. Set Rhubarb.

6th Feb
- Attlee cables Australia for food help. Argentina's relief efforts. Britain to have darker bread. There have been a lot of complaints against Ben Smith's reduction of ration threat of 1oz less bacon. U.N.O. deadlock over Greece continues, back stage talks fail. Mr Beven and Mr. Vyshinsky have private talks. Went to woodwork. The St Leger races will be held at Doncaster Racecourse on Sept 9th, it will be the first time the course has been in use since the war began.

7th Feb
- Tobacco, films, and petrol may be given up for food. Wives plan big protest, they want food from USA instead of films. British troops to stay in Greece. Anglo-Soviet dispute ended. Mr Vyshinsky and Beven shake hands. British summer time comes in on the 14th April. The individual case against Hess starts at Nuremburg today.

8th Feb
- Sir Ben Smith, "We now face more drastic hardships than in the war". Food controls must be tighter says minister, but no more cuts likely yet. There is now only a few days left before U.N.O. closes down. U.N.O. headquarter problem still not decided on yet. Dad has to go to Sheffield about his bad hand tomorrow, he is still off work.

9th Feb
- Very rainy last night and night before, extensive damage done all over country by floods yesterday. Dad went to Sheffield to see Doctor about Beet hand, went to see his cousin just outside the city. Doncaster sets national savings target for £1,000,000 for year beginning April 1st 1946. Pay Day.

10th Feb

- Bill had a cassock and surplice on and sang in the choir at 9:30am and 6:00pm, I pumped church organ and went to Communion.

11th Feb

- U.N.O. now dealing with Indonesian problem. U.S.S.R. charging Nuremburg. The axis invasion and occupation of Yugoslavia brought death to 1,650,000 persons (over 10% of population), Soviet prosecutor told the international war crimes tribunal today. Hitler ordered end of Yugoslavia in 1941.

12th Feb

- Half day. Went to Doncaster Gaumont to see "I'll be seeing you". Missed metalwork. Bill went choir practice and boys club. Rioting going on in Calcutta.

13th Feb

- YMCA club ransacked and its furniture set alight. Troops open fire in Calcutta, 19 killed, 23o wounded. Trains, depot, and post offices wrecked. Compromise on Java, U.N.O. solution likely to be given tonight. Went to woodwork.

14th Feb

- Security Council adjourns after another procedure wrangle. New U.N.O. delay on Syria problem - delegates will be heard tomorrow. Got 10 extra industrial clothing coupons from Green's today. Worked at Green's shop for 12 months today. Death roll in Calcutta fights now 42.

15th Feb

- It is not so easy as it looks keeping a diary for a hole year! Mr Ernest Bevin to make most important speech tomorrow. Britain ready to hand mandates to U. N. O. When reporters asked Churchill how British people were fairing, he said, "The British people will take whatever comes to them". Bill went to second choir practice tonight at 6:30pm.

16th Feb

- Norway calls U.N.O. to end Nazism and Fascism, "Rid world of this poison". Martin Bormann, only uncaptured Nazi leader who became

Hitler's deputy after Hess in 1941 was in his absence accused of being a principal architect of Nazi conspiracy. Today very keen frost, below freezing point, the frost stopped all day, also fog. Got some Jaffa's from Wards. Tony Johnson puts 8/- in club.

17th Feb

- Bevin pledges all our strength to U.N.O. peace drive. Aggressors must be swiftly stopped. Bruce Woodcock to fight Freddie Mills in May. England to Capetown air record by RAF Lancaster, arrives 4hrs ahead of 1939. Rained in night, ice on roads this morning. Churchill now sun-bathing in Miami. Bill brings brass toasting fork home which he made in metalwork (school). Doctor says dads got a Beet hand, may have to go to Doncaster infirmary tomorrow.

18th Feb

- Not so cold this morning but snowed at noon (1st). Stayed all night. Russia argues strong U.N.O. action from start. Critics of charter are dangerous. Bill got 2/6 off Mr. Ward for taking orders.

19th Feb

- More snow this morning, fog at night. Winter will hold over weekend. Outlook - cold and more snow (weather forecast). America's biggest industrial crisis, Pittsburgh steel workers start strike today, New York faced with transport hold-up. (New strike 150,000 men).

20th Feb

- All India now upset. Riots, strikes and hunger strikes continue. Indian ratings beat up British officers. Desert riots after false radio flash (ratings of the Royal Indian Navy are the rioters). Went night school, woodwork.

21st Feb

- Mrs Armitage of Birtley died yesterday, friend of mam. British troops go into action in ugly situation in two countries. Indian service disorders flare up at Bombay. Strong British forces move to storm centres.

22nd Feb

- Apples expected in Rossington on Monday. Tommy Handley made his 200th broadcast last night accompanied by his gang of I.T.M.A.

comedians. Mr. Attlee says British Naval units will reach Bombay soon. Unconditional surrender demand to Indian mutineers. Hopeful sign in Bombay harbour but rebellion on shore. Went pictures to see George Formby in Bell Bottom George. Bill got paid 2/6 off Mr. Ward for taking 3 orders. Dad been off work 6 weeks with beet hand, Dr. gave him 1 more week off.

23rd Feb

- Casualties rise to 1,000 as 200 more Indians killed, tragedy enters fourth day. Mutineers yield but Bombay mob runs amok. "End this orgy", says Ghandi. Rossington lost 2-0 at Football with Stainforth. Workmen have begun to put electric pump in St Luke's church organ.

24th Feb

- Bill and I went to 9:30am Communion, 6:30 Evensong, and at 7:45 to Holy Concert given by male voice choir. Bill in choir for services and I pumped the organ. The collection was to raise money for the electric organ pumper (silver collection). Riots continue in India. Very cold this morning (ice), me and Bill went for a walk over the Mount, Rossington.

25th Feb

- Received book from Oldham's Press (John Bull) which I sent for on 31st Jan (6/3). Got 2lbs of Canadian apples (red) from Green's (1/6) (We had none at Xmas in Rosso. Nazi leader tries to blame Britain for warmongering. Ribbetrop calls on Churchill as a witness. He says that Britain threatened to destroy the Reich and forced Hitler to arms. Bombay now at normal after riots.

26th Feb

- Half day. Went metalwork making screwdriver. Repaired cycle this afternoon. Bill went choir practice and boy's club. School breaks up for 3 day holiday.

27th Feb

- Went night school (woodwork). Spanish dictator forestalls decision to cut him off, General Franco closes frontier to France. Anglo-US moves, will U.N.O. now act.

28th Feb

- Oranges arrive in Rosso. Sudden wheat cut precipitates grave food crisis in British zone of Germany. Monty to tell cabinet of German famine fear as 20,000,000 Germans in the zone. Snow this morning gone by end of day. Went pictures, no good!

1st Mar

- Dad has been off work for 7 weeks with bad hand (the referee at Sheffield said it was not beet hand). Got 2lb of apples and 2lb of oranges from Green's. Zoning is supposed to finish on 2nd March.

2nd Mar

- Arctic weekend for Britain forecast. It was 16 deg below freezing point at Dyce, nr Aberdeen this afternoon. Bruce Woodcock, the Empire heavy weight champion is to fight in USA on May 13th. His opponent is undecided. Had my usual Sat night bath.

3rd Mar

- Snowed heavily all day but did not settle properly as ground was wet. Bill and I went to Holy Communion and to 6:30 service. Bill brought cassock and surplice home to be washed. Ration period number 9 begins today, we get 4 extra points, making the total to 24 each per month, as there is now a bigger variety of points goods. But there is a snag as lard goes down from 2oz to 1oz. Franco is now in the news very much.

4th Mar

- Went to ENSA concert a welfare hall (9d). Cabinet discusses crisis over red army garrisons in Persia. Britain considers action in face of Soviet treaty breach, Moscow asked to explain.

5th Mar

- Pancake Day, half day holiday. Went to picture house (Don). Went metalwork and finished screwdriver (2d). Bill attended choir practice.

6th Mar

- Mended chair at woodwork for Mrs. Green. Finished my aircraft carrier (1/-)

7th Mar

- Went pictures (Home in Indonesia). Got 2s off Mrs. Green for mending chair. Wrote letter to Peg. Lemons in Rosso, canned fruit expected this week, no bananas yet (patience).

8th Mar

- Pointer came to see us; this is his first leave since he joined up. Ray knocked all next doors fence out, Dad apologised (other nips helped him). Bill finished garden rake at school today, (5d). Dad has been off work for 8 weeks but starts on Monday (afternoons for 6 weeks). Oil boring is now starting at Gringley-on-the-hill near Doncaster.

9th Mar

- Crowd of up to 60-70,000 see greatest disaster in Britain's football history. More than 500 injured and 33 people lost their lives at Bolton Wanderers and Stoke City FA Cup tie at Burnden Park, Bolton, when 2 barriers near a stand gave way. Nine men lay unidentified. I've got a bad cold but went work, I will have day in tomorrow. Had suet pudding for sweet at dinner time (good).

10th Mar

- Missed church, got a touch of flu. Police investigating the fire which broke out in the 88,000 ton Queen Elizabeth docked in Southampton were last night convinced it was the work of saboteurs.

11th Mar

- Dad starts work on afternoons. Green's get some imitation fat called Snortal 1/10 per lb.

12th Mar

- Half day. Went metalwork and mended small cycle and barrow wheel. Had haircut. Bill attended choir practice. 4,000 workers are on strike at the Humber car works in Coventry, and 12,000 at the Ford works in Sussex.

13th Mar

- Went woodwork, made baking board. Had 3 punctures in my order bike. J. G. Bestall to be new manager of Doncaster Rovers football team. Goering goes to witness stand at Nuremburg. Starts story of his career. Russian Garrisons. Persian premier says he protested to Stalin. Mystery of Red Army's move into country, possible lever in internal affairs. Green's get some tinned fruit in.

14th Mar

- Had 4/6 tips. Strikes continue in Coventry. Stalin attacks Mr. Churchill about his speech which he made in USA.

15th Mar

- Got a 2/3 cake from Green's also 1/- worth of loose Horlicks. Dad finishes his first week at pit for 8 weeks. Crescent fish shop closes down, under new management next week. Bread is now very dark. Bill went pictures to see Syd Howard in Up for the Cup. I saved my money 1/-. Churchill replies to Stalin.

16th Mar

- I am beginning to get fed up of messing around at Green's, pay day still £1. India free to choose one rule within or without of the empire says Mr.Attlee.

17th Mar

- Bill and I went to Communion and the Evensong. Ray attended Sunday school.

18th Mar

- Banana's in Rossington next week says Peter's (fruit merchant). Bill went pictures and I went down about 6:30pm but could not get in. arliamentarians may have £500 tax free spend allowance. Pay increase to £1,000 for MP's, that is not a professional salary.

19th Mar

- Rosso boys school play Edlington school in semi-final for the cup (at Edlington) and win 5-2. Half day, missed metalwork, went pictures (whistling in Brooklyn). Charles' birthday aged 2 years. Bill went choir practice.

20th Mar

- Went woodwork and started to make plate rack. Received birthday card to Charles from Peg.

21st Mar

- Grapefruit arrive in Rosso 7d a lb. Mr Bevin outlines free-for-all health service bill. 1948 suggested as the starting date, national medical scheme will cost £152,000,000 yearly. Everyone in England will come under this scheme. Today is the beginning of Spring. Crescent fish shop opens under new management. Started putting odd coppers in tin, see how much in at Xmas.

22nd Mar

- The ministry of food announces today that there will be cuts in lard and soap very shortly, but not until Sir Ben Smith reports. Pumped church organ for crucifiction practice. Peg sends parcel of oranges and biscuits.

23rd Mar

- Went to church hall to see the pantomime ("the Queen of Hearts") produced by the church youth club, it was very good (went in 4pm came out 10:30pm). Pegs birthday aged 24, did not send present as Dad has been off work and were are short of money. mean to send one later on. Rosso senior boys lose Daily Dispatch Cup to Skellow 3-1.

24th Mar

- Me and Bill went to 9:30 am Communion and 6:30 pm evensong. The preacher was the priest of new Edlington. Sir Ben smith says US are playing the game with regards to the food shortage. Sir Ben, Food Minister, brought better news for British housewives (back from US). He is starting an enquiry to discover what prompted the statement that there would be a cut in margarine and soap ration, he denied any knowledge of it. Very sunny.

25th Mar

- Had letter from Peg to say that she will be here on Friday 26th. 432,000 bananas arrive in Doncaster, they are now in the ripening house and Rossington will get its allocation on Thursday (I hope). Lovely and sunny this morning, when it's like this my job is like a holiday (on the bike).

26th Mar

- Half day. Went metalwork, started to make blazer (fire). Bought new handle grips for Bill's cycle (rubber 9d). Charles alls on tar and cuts his leg, also fell downstairs. Telephoned to Green's Boswell Road this morning, that is the fourth time I have phoned. Bill went pictures. Zoning of food etc. finished on March 2nd but so far I can see no change in our shops.

27th Mar

- Went woodwork. Bill went pictures. He got 1/10 tips at wards

28th Mar

- Our family see a banana for the first time for 6 (long) years. Ray and Charles have seen them for the first time in their life. Green's got 2 cases of bananas this morning and 2 more will come in on Monday. They gave me one to bring home, we all had a bite.

29th Mar

- Pumped church organ. Peg comes home on demobilisation leave 56 days. Bought Dad snap tin 1/6.

30th Mar

- Pay day still £1. Bruce Woodcock beat George James in the third round last night at Hull. He submitted after being battered badly.

31st Mar

- Mothering Sunday. 70 attended Holy Communion at 9:30 this morning (Bill in choir, I pumped). We also attended 6:30 Evensong. The Rector J. M. Shaw preached. Me and Bill set some seeds, Radish and Beetroot.

1st Apr

- 2nd part of number one allocation of banana's arrived in Rosso today; this lot is properly ripened (3 cases). Peg buys Charles toy train.

2nd Apr

- Mrs. Green let me have 2lbs of bananas (off book 2.2d). Peg cut Mam's hair. Bill had day off school to go to Doncaster with me and Peg, he had his photo took at Woolworths (six for 6/-), in his cassock and surplice (choir). Peg got hers took too. Went metalwork and finished Blazer (1/3). Started shoe horn (brass). Flat racing starts today.

3rd Apr

- Langton Abbot wins Lincoln races today 7-1. Went woodwork. Got 3lb of bananas from Mr. Ward and 1lb of Cunar. Wash day. Rovers (Don) beat Stockport 4-1 this afternoon.

4th Apr

- Petriot, the French blue beard who murdered 67 people was sentenced to death today.

5th Apr

- Went comunicans guild. Lovely Cottage wins Grand National, Jack Finley second, and Prince Regent third (was favourite). Got cream cake from Green's. Peg got Bill's photo's (6), from Doncaster

6th Apr

- Pay day. Doncaster boys win York boys 4-1 at Rossington this afternoon.

7th Apr

- Went church morning communion at 6:30 evensong. Was paid 10s for pumping organ for 3 months. Baily (Rector of Armthorpe) preached at 6:30 Evensong. Bill missed choir this morning because he had pains, went at night.

8th Apr

- Bruce Woodcock wins Bert Gilorey, Scottish Heavyweight, in 4 minutes and 10 seconds of boxing (2 rounds). Bruce goes to U.S. on Friday. Went for coal for Mr. Green (1s for bringing it).

9th Apr

- Painted Bill's bike silver and black. Went metalwork and finished brass shoe horn. Mr Hugh Dalton gives his budget tonight

10th Apr

- Last night purchase tax was taken off nearly all needed articles, pots, pans, blankets etc. Lower entertainment tax on all sport but horse, motor, and dog racing. Income tax goes up from 1/10 to 1/8 (not felt until October). Went woodwork.

11th Apr

- Dad fills in papers for family allowance which starts in August, 5/1 for each child after the first if they are not working. Went pictures with Bill to see 'Escape to Happiness', Ingrid Bergman and Lesley Howard.

12th Apr

- Bruce Woodcock (boxer) goes to America today (we all wish him good luck). Rossington Parish Council will provide a meal for every Rossington child on Victory Day, June 8th. Summer time begins at 2am on Sunday. All clocks in Britain will be put back 1 hour. Today is the anniversary of Mr. Roosevelt's death; he died a year ago today. Peg went Staffs.

13th Apr

- Bill got pair of new pants today. Bill painted bike wheels silver (and spoilt it!). Pay day £1.

14th Apr

- Palm Sunday, me Bill and Ray got palm crosses and went church at 9:30am. 6:30pm he vicar of Blythe preached, he said we had a wonderful choir. Sold Tony a knife for 2/6.

15th Apr

- Put £1-10 in school bank. Went woodwork and finished plate rack (10d). Dad on afternoons this week.

16th Apr

- Metalwork finishes tonight until next year (I am not going). Dad came home from pit (0 of them had to change stalls so they all came home). Mam went pictures for the first time in about 2 years; me and Bill looked after Charles. She went with Dad. Opencast coalmining has started on the Wentworth Woodhouse Estate owned by Earl Fitzwilliam. His plea to stop it was rejected. Doncaster race course is now ready for the St. Leger.

17th Apr
- Pumped church organ for crucifixion (Colin Robson helped me). There was a bit of excitement when the electric lights went out and the singers had to sing by candle light. Two men (strangers) took the solo parts; there is another performance in the chapel tomorrow. Bill went pictures. Rain came down in bucket-loads this evening. Bruce Woodcock will fight Tami Mauriello on May 13th.

18th Apr
- Tomatoes arrive in Rossington (Greens) (Canary Islands) 1s 4d lb.

19th Apr
- Good Friday. Had no fish or hot cross buns. Bill went church for a total of 5 hours, 2 hours devotion 1pm to 3pm, and 1 hour service from 8pm to 9pm (in choir). Dad came back from pit this afternoon, bit of trouble over promised money, second time this week. All men came back. Green's shop will close on Easter Monday.

20th Apr
- Got a new pair of trousers (pin-striped grey). Mr. Green gave me 5s for an Easter present; he also let me have 1lb of tomatoes (1/4). Me and Bill went pictures to see 'Hey Rookie'.

21st Apr
- Easter Sunday! Me and Bill attended 9:30am Communion and 6:30pm Evensong, the choir sang their anthem 'King of Kings'. Bill also attended 3:15pm choir practice. We had stewed rhubarb, rhubarb pie and egg custard pie for tea.

22nd Apr
- Easter Monday! Whole day off from Greens; stopped at home.

23rd Apr
- Half day. Took Bill to Doncaster and bought some plastic wire, it's now a craze in Rosso making bangles and hair bands with it (2d per yard). Went Ritz to see 'Forest Rangers', also had strawberry milkshake (6d)

at Elite cafe and a cup of coffee and three chocolate biscuits at Bus Station Cafe.

24th Apr

- Went pictures to see 'Tom Sawyer', (an inspiration, a real good picture!). During the war the Germans lost 1,110 submarines.

25th Apr

- The Governments wheat economy plans will be out tomorrow. Mam and Dad went pictures to see 'Tom Sawyer', by Mark Twain. Had 2/0 tips.

26th Apr

- Went pictures to see 'When Irish eyes are smiling'. Loaves will soon be cut down from 2lbs to 1¾lbs. The price will remain the same (4½d). Peg went to Chesterfield.

27th Apr

- Pay day £1.

28th Apr

- Bill went 9:30 Communion (I missed). Bill and I went 6:30 Evensong. Paid paper man. Ration period #11 begins today.

29th Apr

- Joe Pine came to see us, he is a Lance Corporal. He will shortly go to Africa. He will then be made a Sergeant Instructor. Went to E.N.S.A. concert. Number 2 allocation of bananas arrives in Rosso.

30th Apr

- Bill and Ray start school today after 1½ weeks Easter holiday. Went Doncaster with Peg; also went pictures to see 'Caravan'. There was a man killed at pit today!

1st May

- Not a bad day for the 1st of May. Dr. Alan Nunn, an atomic expert and lecturer in physics at King's College, London, was sentenced to 10 years penal servitude for communicating information contrary to the Official Secrets Act 1911 (he gave information to the Russian's). There is a procession carnival on May the 4th (Sat), also a May Queen.

2nd May

- Bob Hughes has been elected (chairman) councillor for Rosso for the 15th time. Bill attended choir practice.

3rd May

- Went pictures to see 'Murder in Reverse', mam and dad also went.

4th May

- Peg went back to her peace-time job (domestic service) to Lechworth, Nr London at 10 to 8 this morning. There was a May Day procession this afternoon; all the nips go was a free punch and judy show. Dad won 19s 3d on two horses today, the first he's backed for a long time.

5th May

- Bill and I attended 9:30am communion and 6:30pm evensong

6th May

- The Bruce Woodcock V Tami Meuriello fight has been postponed until May 14th ($ days). Bread goes down a quarter of a pound in weight today, you can't tell much difference. The second part of number 2 allocation of bananas came to Green's today. I got 2lb. Dad on afters. Had letter from Peg. £937,000,000 from America may be approved this week; U.S. hopes revive, but Britain ready for 'No'.

7th May

- Half day. Got coal in (1 ton). Went pictures to see James Mason in 'Mill on the Floss'. Bill went choir practice, afterwards he attended a meeting of the choir, they are going to Filey on pit week.

8th May

- Had bath. Wash day. All British forces are to withdraw from Egypt (it will take about 2 years). Doncaster boys won York boys 8-1 yesterday at York; they play Bradford or Rotherham for the final on Saturday. A year ago today the war in Europe ended (VE Day).

9th May

- America has rejected the loan to Britain; the votes were 46 against and 40 in favour. Mr Morrison will go to see President Truman on Saturday for urgent food talks (Washington).

10th May

- Went to pictures to see George Formby in 'I Didn't Do It'. Mr Morrison flew to U.S. today. Fred Mills will fight Gus Lesvenich (World Cruiser Weight Campion) on Tuesday next.

11th May

- Rotherham boys won Doncaster boys in the North England Cup 1-0 (Wylie).

12th May

- Bill and I attended 9:30am communion and 6:30pm evensong. Mr Roebuck asked me to go to Filey, I said yes.

13th May

- Went to pictures. Yorkshire miners may come out on strike in a fortnight.

14th May

- Ray, Terrence, and Alan bought matches and made a fire at the side of the church hall (they could smell it inside). Mrs Roebuck caught them and they all had to stay in at playtime.

15th May

- Fred Mills lost the fight against Gus Lesvenich in 10th round. Went to pictures to see 'Grenwich Village'. It rained today, first time for about 3 weeks. Wireless licenses will go up from 10s to £1 on June 1st.

16th May

- Started summer class night school (metalwork). Making brass-handled poker. You will be able to change your grocer every 8 weeks beginning Sept 1st, also your butcher, but not Milkman.

17th May

- Bruce Woodcock fights tomorrow at 3:15am B.S.T., 10:15pm tonight U.S. time.

18th May

- Tami Mauriello beats Bruce Woodcock in 5th round Knock Out. Bruce needs more experience says Jack Dempsey. The contest was watched by 13,749 people, he was winning on points to the 5th round (he had a cut on the head which he received when he collided with Mauriello five minutes before knock-out, which may have caused his defeat), 4 stitches. We were all very disappointed.

19th May

- Empire Youth Sunday. Bill and I attended church at 9:30am and 6:30pm. Went for a walk over Mount with Bill

20th May

- Went pictures.

21st May

- Half day. Stopped in. Bill went choir practice.

22nd May

- Dad got £1, Peg's war gift from Welfare Hall (she gave it him).

23rd May

- Went metalwork and started jam spoon.

24th May

- We get our new ration on May 28th.

25th May

- Mam and Dad went to pictures. Pay Day £1.

26th May

- Missed church this morning but attended 6:30pm evensong. Queen Mary is 49 today. Point period 12 starts today.

27th May

- Went to E.N.S.A. concert at Welfare Hall 9d it was rotten. Bill went pictures.

28th May

- Got new ration books from Welfare Hall which means 1 more year of rationing at least. Started cleaning teeth. Sir Ben Smith, Minister of Food resigns. Went pictures to see 'Echo Murders'.

29th May

- Received letter from Doncaster Co-op department (joinery) asking me to be present for an interview at 10am tomorrow. Went pictures with Dad.

30th May

- Got up at 7am and caught 9am bus to Doncaster, was at the old co-op Don at 9:35am. Had interview at 10:05am (interview about 2 minutes). Had trifle and ice-cream at Woolworths and had a look round the store. Caught 10:45am bus, back at Green's 11:30am. I will get to know later if I get the job (apprentice joiner). 8 boys applied. Attended metalwork.

31st May

- Plans are ready for bread rationing in Britain (just in case). We will know if it will be rationed by end of June. Found a ball down old village. Got 4 ton of grit at Green's.

The Echo Murders

1st June

- Pay day £1. Mr Green gave me 2/6 for myself. Went pictures to see 'Within these Walls'. Wireless licenses increased to £1 today.

2nd June

- Bill and I attended church for 9:30am communion and 6:30pm evensong. Filled in ration books.

3rd June

- Got an egg out of swallows nest in our house (4 left in). Bruce Woodcock fights Freddie Mills tomorrow night.

4th June

- Bruce Woodcock fights Freddie Mills at 9:30pm tonight.

5th June

- 'Airborn' (50-1) won the first Derby to be held at Epsom Downs, 'Gulf Stream' was 2nd favourite, and 'Radiotherapy 3rd. Dad backed 'Khaled' which came 4th. Bruce Woodcock won Freddie Mills on points last night (12 rounds), they share £10,000. Ray got V card from King's school.

6th June

- Went metalwork.

7th June

- Finished work until Tuesday and have the 8th off for V Day, and Monday 10th off for Whitsuntide.

8th June

- Victory Day today. A great V-Parade was held in London (rained), firework display at night, the parade was broadcast. Went sports 1/6. A small circus came to Rosso, Bill went 1s 1d (Rotten). Bill and I went to pictures to see 'Thunderhead - Son of Flicka'.

9th June

- Bill and I attended church at 9:30am and 6:30pm. Bill and Ray go to Roche Abbey with church boys (Bill on Wed and Ray on Thurs)

10th June

- Whit Monday. Bill and I went to Doncaster. Went pictures.

11th June
- Jack Johnson died in hospital today (aged 68 yrs, negro), world champion boxer 1908-15 (road accident). Bill and I went for a walk half way to Doncaster (poured with rain).

12th June
- Syd Howard died today (comedian film star), heart failure. Went to pictures. Bill went to Roche Abbey with church. Number 3 allocation of bananas arrives

13th June
- Got 2s tips. Missed metalwork, holiday for Whit.

14th June
- Got tin of Prem

15th June
- Pay day, Cyril Green gave me 2/-.

16th June
- Bill and I attended 9:30am communion and 6:30pm evensong.

17th June
- Joe Louis fights Bill Coin on Wednesday at the Yankee Stadium.

18th June
- Went Doncaster with Dad and applied for a job as a Telegraph Boy with LNER as I have heard nothing of my other job (joiner). Went pictures to see 'Beloved Enemy'.

19th June
- There was an accident at Rossington level crossing last night when the trucks broke through the gates and carried a car 50 yds down the line. The driver was Mr Cook, Newsagent from Rosso. He only suffered from shock, but Mr Guest took him to the hospital at Doncaster.

20th June
- Just got new bottle of ink. Joe Louis wins Billy Coin at the Yankee Stadium. Joe Louis retained his world heavy weight title when he knocked Coin out in the 8th round. Went metalwork.

21st June
- Went pictures with Bill to see 'Meet me in St. Louis'.

22nd June

- Pay day and Cyril gave me 2/-. Mam and Dad went to pictures and Dad slept in for work. Dug garden over. Bread ration books ready says food minister (photo in this morning's paper), the ration will be about 10 oz each but extra for heavy workers and children.

23rd June

- Bill and I attended communion (Bill felt faint and came out in middle of service). I went myself to 6:30pm evensong. Bread ration is now certain says food minister. Very hot this morning but thunderstorms in afternoon. Points period 13 starts today and soap is cut by one seventh from today.

24th June

- Bill went pictures and Dad went to draw £5 out of bank.

25th June

- Half day. Got some new shoes and trousers for holidays. Took Ray to the pictures to see' Waltz Time'. England beat India by 10 wickets in their test match today. Number 4 allocation of bananas arrived yesterday (1lb for under 18's). Bill went to choir practice.

26th June

- I received a letter from Doncaster LNER asking if I would attend at the superintendants office on Friday 28th for a medical examination for the job I applied for a week ago on Tuesday. Bill and I attended a meeting at the church hall, Mr Shaw (old village Rector) and Mr Roebuck were discussing the problems which arose from the party going to Filey (camping), and there will be 40 at the camp, 10s for Bill and 25s for me. We set off by train from Rossington at 7:45am (food was the biggest problem). The Food Minister, Mr Stracney (who has just arrived from Canada) says there is no immediate relief for Britain's food plight. The cabinet will decide tomorrow if bread will be rationed or not.

27th June

- Bread is to be rationed on the 21st July. Went pictures to see 'This Man's Navy' with Bill.

28th June

- Went to Doncaster for an interview and medical examination (colour blind tests etc.). I will know if I have passed sometime next week. Races begin at Doncaster, first for 7 years, it looked just like a pre-war race meeting as I passed in the bus this morning (it was not the St. Leger).

29th June

- There was an accident in old Rossington this afternoon when a light Ford van collided with the red Doncaster bus, one man was killed and three were taken to hospital (Bill saw the accident). Uncle Ted came round later. One more has died since. Bill went Doncaster races with Alb Draper (there was long queues at the bus stands for the races). Pay day £1. Cyril Green gave me 2s. The American atom tests (on ships) will be carried out at 10:30am tomorrow.

30th June

- Bill and I missed church this morning but attended 6:30pm evensong, I went cycle ride to Blyth, 15 miles (7½ each way), had a look around the Abbey which was built in 1088. George Hedley (uncle 16yrs old) came down for 6 week holiday yesterday.

1ˢᵗ July

- Cut Mam's hair. Went pictures with Bill to see 'A Bell for Adona'.

2ⁿᵈ July

- Dad went to Leeds on business for colliery. Bill, Mam, Charlie, and I went to Doncaster. Bill got a new suit £9-7s-6d from Surge, I got a pair of pyjamas 10s-3d.

3ʳᵈ July

- Bread debate begins in parliament.

4ᵗʰ July

- Received letter from LNER, IVE GOT THE JOB! I will go to Doncaster tomorrow for particulars. Missed school, took clothes over to church for camp on Saturday (also food).

5ᵗʰ July

- My last day at Green's. Went to Doncaster LNER office to get particulars about my new job! I am to start work at 9am a week on Monday. Left Green's at 6pm, he gave me one week's holiday with pay and 10/- for myself (he is a good man). From 6pm to 7:30pm we were all fussing about getting ready (packing) for holidays (Bill and I). Got hair cut.

6ᵗʰ July

- Got up at 5:30am and caught the 7:56am train for Doncaster. Changed for Bridlington at 9:15am and arrived in Brid at 10:35am. Caught first sight of sea at 12:15 (Reighton). Had dinner at 1 o'clock. Sunny day, went on beach. Mr Shaw, Rector will look after camp until Wednesday when Mr. Roebuck takes over. Went to Filey from Reighton 9d return.

7ᵗʰ July

- Stopped in Reighton and went bathing. Seven lads went sun bathing this morning, now four of them are in bed bandaged up, I am just a little sore.

8ᵗʰ July

- Got up at 3:30am (saw sun rise), walking along beach at 4am, breakfast at 6:30am. Howard, Bill, and I went to Scarborough (2/-) Got 5 sticks of rock and a book 1/9d, had good day. Mr. Fawcett, my old school master died today. Went to Bridlington with two lads and went fishing (4/- for 2 hours), caught whiting (9inch), told skipper we would see him tomorrow at 6:30am, so five of us planned to get up at 3am and walk to Bridlington (8 miles).

9th July

- One of the lads stopped up all night and woke us at 3am, we made cocoa, took a tomato, 2 biscuits, and a piece of cake each, and set off walking at 3:15am (woke no-one). Arrived in Bridlington at 5:35am with very sore feet. Got cup of tea at fishermen's cafe (open 5am), sailed out at 6:30am on large motorboat. Fished for 2 hours but caught no fish. Made me feel a little sick (another 4 bob), enjoyed ourselves. Came home at 1pm just in time to do my turn at dinner duties. Bill went to Flamborough Head on lorry with other lads.

10th July

- Went to Scarborough with Jack Dyson, had photo took (2/9), spent up all but 3 bob. Mam and family went Skegness.

11th July

- Gave Bill last 3/- to go to Scarborough with 2 other lads, he bought mam a brooch out of it. altogether we bought Ray falling bricks 1s-11d, story book 3s- 11d, and a few small things, Mam a brooch 1s- 6d, Pot dog 4s-6d, won some earrings 3d, Dad, a pipe 3s-6d, a handkerchief 8s-½d, Charlie, a spade 2s-6d, hankie 1s-4d.

12th July

- Had a lovely week and ready for home (me and Bill spent £4). Home lovely and brown at 5pm and ready for new job on Monday (14th). Mam, Ray, and Charles, enjoyed their holiday to Skegness very much, Ray went on a boat on a very sunny day. Still got 2 bad blisters which I got from walking to Bridlington on Wednesday (9th).

13th July

- Had headache so stopped off church this morning, went 6:30pm evensong. Bread goes on ration next Sunday (20th). The American loan goes through, it will partly end austerity. I start my new job tomorrow.

14th July

- STARTED WORK at the LNER School learning Morse code, I've learned it in the first day; I'm learning to be a telegraph boy. Went to pictures to see 'Latin Quarter' with Bill.

15th July

- I am now sending Morse from an instrument (tapping it).

16TH July

- Rain for third time this week. Bruce Woodcock will fight Albert Renet of France for the European title on July 29th.

17th July

- I was very disappointed tonight when all the other lads got paid and I found out that I had to work 1 week in hand.

18th July

- A bit of good news, I get my bus fare paid so wages will be £1 14s wages and 4s bus fare.

19th July

- Half day, finished at 11:30am. Came home, had dinner, and went back to Doncaster at 2:30pm. Queued for 15 minutes for some Wall's Ice-cream and went to the pictures at the Ritz. The Bakers battle has been lost. Circular from HQ urges them to work bread rationing scheme, feeling government may back down said Mr Fred Philips of Bradford (Chairman of the Union of Bakers).

20th July

- Bread rationing and the new ration books start today (period 1). Went church 9:30am communion and 6:30pm evensong. All cereal food stuffs go on points. Oatmeal, semolina, etc.

21st July

- Begin 2nd week at my new job. I've got a very sore tongue. British GHQ blown up, 10 killed, many (60) injured by bomb in Jerusalem, YMCA damaged, deputy commissioner had a narrow escape.

22nd July

- 42 injured, 52 dead, and 72 missing are the latest figures of Jerusalem bomb plot.

23rd July

- Lost 2/6 going to work. Got my LNER badge (No E 48006).

24th July

- 121 official death roll in Jerusalem bomb plot. (42 injured).

25th July

- Pay day, first on my new job!! Got £1 15s.

26th July

- Doncaster had worst rain for 40 years this afternoon (I came home in it). Went to pictures with Bill.

27th July

- Half day, Bill and I went to Gaumont to see 'The Spanish Main'.

28th July

- Special Sunday services for children. Bill and I attended 9:30am communion and 6:30pm evensong (I still pump the organ). Bruce Woodcock fight Albert Renet (France) for the European title tomorrow 29th at Belle View. Bertram & Mills circus is at Doncaster and opens tomorrow.

29th July

- Bruce Woodcock knocked Albert Renet out in the sixth round at Belle View for the European title; he will now fight Gus Lesnovich on Setember 17th (London).

30th July

- 16,000 British troops combing out Palestine's. All-Jew city saw troops pounce on Tel-Aviv, to shoot if curfew is broken. Terrorists responsible for King David bomb plot.

31st July

- Bill gets school report (top), good. Mother receives family allowance book 10s per week.

1st Aug

- British troops arrest 664 suspects for Jerusalem bomb plot in Tel Aviv. Schools break up for summer holidays (6 weeks).

2nd Aug

- Pay day £1 14s 4d wage. Bill met me at the circus (racecourse Doncaster). We stood from 5pm til 7pm and managed to get a good seat. The circus was good and we enjoyed ourselves, (Bertram and Mills circus).

3rd Aug

- Dad took Ray to the circus. Half day, finished work at 12:30 until Tuesday for August bank holiday (with pay).

4th Aug

- Bill attended 9:30am communion. Bill and I attended 6:30pm evensong. Mam starts drawing family allowance on Tuesday.

5th Aug

- Bank holiday Monday. Millions flock to the sea-sides (in greater numbers than in 1939). I made a quiet day of it and went to pictures at Rossington in the evening. Bill went to boating lake (Wheatley Hills). Holiday with pay.

6th Aug

- Family allowance begins and mother draws 10/- from post office. Oranges arrive in Rosso, first for a time.

7th Aug

- Went for a ride with Tony.

8th Aug

- Went to pictures to see 'The Great Flamingo'.

9th Aug

- I was tested at work on receiving Morse, I got 7⅕ per minute, other lad got 5.6.3. Pay day got £2 1s wages (including bus fare). Bruce Woodcock flies to Sweden.

10th Aug

- Half day, went Rossington pictures to see 'Son of Lassie'.

11th Aug
- Bill and I attended 9:30am communion and 6:30pm evensong. Bill and I went walk to Sheep Dip Corner. Bill and I went pea picking and earned 5s 7½d (with Mark).

12th Aug
- Went pictures to see 'Gentle Annie' with Tony. (words received 8⅔).

13th Aug
- Freddie Mills fights Jon Lettel (Sweden) tonight. Family allowance day, mother draws her 10/-.

14th Aug
- Freddie knocked out Jon Lettel from Sweden in the 1st round last night after 2 minutes 59 seconds, he was down twice. Went to pictures to see George Formby in 'Nothing to Say', (nothing else to do).

15th Aug
- The food offices announced on Monday that left over BU's (bread units) can be exchanged for points, since then thousands at the food offices (photo's of queues in paper).

16th Aug
- Pay day £1 17s.

17th Aug
- Half day. Yorkshire action to stop sale of 1d coupon (bread).

18th Aug
- Bill attended 9:30am communion and 6:30pm evensong

19th Aug
- Bread ration has been a success, 109,000 tons of wheat saved in the first month. Palestine campaign of terror planned today, seized documents betray biggest Jewish plot. 50,000 British troops are ready and the guard will be doubled on all public buildings.

20th Aug
- Went pictures. Got some ink. Received over 14 words at work.

21st Aug
- Fair comes to Rossington.

22nd Aug
- No entry.

23rd Aug

- Pay day £1 17s 8d. We will get bigger newspapers from September 23rd (6 pages instead of 4, only for 3 days out of each week.

24th Aug

- Met Mam and Dad at Doncaster bus stand and went to Burton to be measured, I picked a navy-blue suit which will cost 5s 15d. Half day so went fair with bill (Dodgems).

25th Aug

- Bill's birthday aged 14 years. Peg sent him 2/6 and a card, Mam and Dad 2/6 and a card, and I gave him 2/-. Went to church this morning but came back home as organ was out of order (and had no breakfast). Mr Roebuck (parson) goes away on 3 weeks holiday.

26th Aug

- Went pictures to see 'Don't Fence Me In'. Beginning 7th week at work.

27th Aug

- Bill attended choir practice. Doncaster racecourse is now in grand form for the St. Leger meeting, Princess Elizabeth will attend with others of the Royal Family. Went to Library.

28th Aug

- Poured down with rain. 50 mph gales sweep the coasts, it will spoil most of the crops. Got weighed at Woolworths 9st 12lb.

29th Aug

- Went pictures. Football season begins on Saturday.

30th Aug

- Pay day £1 17s 8d. Yorkshire cricket team beaten by 10 wickets, first defeat since August 1939. Hampshire triumphs at Bournemouth.

31st Aug

- Half day. I went to have a look at bridge and Balby junction signal boxes with boss, the other lads went to other boxes. Today is the last day of the Nuremburg trial, Goering shouts his innocence. Last day excuses at Nuremburg. Franz said we turned from God and we were doomed. Hess said if he had his life again he would do the same. Doncaster Rovers beat Rochdale 2-1 in their first match this year (at home). Bill and I went to pictures to see 'Perfect Stranger'. Mam and Dad went to see '1st House'; it was a really good picture.

Princess Elizabeth aged 16

1st Sept

- Nazi chiefs wait for their day of judgement - 23rd September! Bill went to church.

2nd Sept

- Mr Cotton, our boss said that 4 of us boys would be going into signal boxes either next week or the week after, (I can still keep in front of the other lads at reading Morse). Went to the pictures.

3rd Sept

- (India) British troops open fire in India. Reinforcements for Bombay, ten killed and forty hurt in third day of brawls. The government are now searching for a plan to tax betting, attempt to find workable scheme.

4th Sept

- Received 15 words a minute today (Morse code)(Most yet!). 150 have been killed in the recent riots, the situation is now quieter.

5th Sept

- Bill has been wearing long trousers for a week!

6th Sept

- Pay day £1 17s 8d. Men on Doncaster market are selling stockings 1d a pair (3 coupons), the make their profit from selling the coupons on the black market at 2/6d each.

7th Sept

- Half day. Betting will not be allowed on the free course at Doncaster on Leger week. 'Airborne', Derby winner is the favourite. The track is now in grand shape, there are 82 toll gates compared with 72 in pre-war. It is reported that Princess Elizabeth is engaged to Prince Philip of Greece, (it is not official).

8th Sept

- Dad and Bill went to church.

9th Sept

- Went to pictures. This week is St. Leger week. The Leger will be run on Wednesday. 'Airborne', Derby winner is the favourite.

10th Sept

- Thousands flock to see first race of Leger week, it's the first for 8 years.

11th Sept

- Leger Day. You could not move in Doncaster this afternoon. 'Airborne', Derby winner and the favourite wins! I was stuck in the crowd outside the course from 5pm until 6pm, I could hardly move. Our bus stops outside the course during this week, after that I had to walk home (home 7 o'clock. Record crowds expected. A dull day but no rain.

12th Sept

- Went to the pictures. 599,000 attend races today (paid). Mr Armitage visited us.

13th Sept

- Last day of races, Dad backs a winner. Pay day £1 17s 8d.

14th Sept

- Mr Cotton told me to report to the Y.M.O. (Yard Masters office) to start work in a signal-box on Monday. I have been in the school for 9 weeks. Half day, went to the pictures. Dad went to work, an extra shift.

15th Sept

- Dad and Bill attended church. 5 squatters leaders arrested in London conspiring to incite trespass on a property. Charge - they have been allowed out on bail. Yesterday was the 6th anniversary of the Battle of Britain. Wrote a letter to Peg.

16th Sept

- Mt first day in a signal-box. It is called 'Red Bank'. I did a little booking (trains), and answered the telephone a few times; I will start on afternoons tomorrow for the rest of the week (2pm until 10pm). Bruce Woodcock fights Gus Lesvenich tomorrow.

17th Sept

- Bruce Woodcock beats Lesvenich in 8th round; K.O. Joe Louis defends his title against Tami Maurillo tomorrow. Worked my first shift on afters' today.

18th Sept
- Tami Maurillo will fight Bruce Woodcock again if he loses the fight tonight with against Joe Louis (which is certain).

19th Sept
- Joe Louis knocked out Tami Maurillo in the first round in New York last night after 2 minutes.

20th Sept
- Pay day £1 17s 8d. Rain during night floods all north England.

21st Sept
- No half day now that I am in a signal-box, and no extra pay, I don't even get my bus fares as before which brings my wage down 4/- but it is a good job.

22nd Sept
- Harvest Festival celebrated today (although it is the worst for about 30 years). Bill and Dad attended church. I start day shift tomorrow, 6am until 2pm.

23rd Sept
- Day shift for the first time in my life, I will have to get up at 4am in a morning for a full week out of every 3! Had all afternoon off and did not feel tires (got up at 3:45am). Ray, Bill, and I went to the pictures to see 'Tarzan's Secret Treasure'. As of today, newspapers will have 6 pages instead of the old 4 page paper; the increased paper will be published 3 days out of each week. Doncaster Rovers are still top of their league (3). They beat Carlisle United 3-2.

24th Sept
- Bread rationing may last 5 more weeks (it was expected to end on 12th October). We bought Charlie a suit from Dolly Spencer for 10/- (hat, leggings, and coat). Miners leaders ask for extra rations of meat for the miners (Stachey will consider it, they need it). I am learning my new job in the signal-box very well; I have not been late since I started at the telegraph school. There was another attempt to break the 17 day old jet record of 616 mph (the plane was damaged). Family allowance pay 10/-.

25th Sept

- Joe Pine came to see us, he is on Embarkation leave (he is going to India). He is one of the squatters at Wadworth (village near here). The world air speed record was not broken in the attempt yesterday, the speed reached was 614 mph (the record is 616). Bill started night school, woodwork and metalwork; he is making a wooden spoon. Just starting to feel the effects of getting up at 4am in the morning, I was very tired this afternoon and went to bed from 3pm until 6:45pm. I now have to write ten lines each day in my diary or I will not fill it by the end of the year, I am going to have a good try.

26th Sept

- 135 people have been killed in air crashes this month (6 Dakota aircraft make up most of the crashed planes). Went to the pictures. 2nd six-page paper issued this week. Underground miners are to get extra meat (a promise) but they are not sure.

27th Sept

- Pay day £1 13s 8d, don't get bus fare paid now. Heath murderer of 2 women was sentenced to death yesterday; there has been nothing but the Heath case in the paper for the last week. I applied for extra rations today (you get 1lbs of sugar, 2 tins of milk, ½ tea per month from the LNER), they said I would have to wait for some tele-girl leaving, but I still use as much tea and stuff as the others, another unfair thing is stopping paying my bus fare. While in the telegraph school I worked 30½ hrs per week and brought £1 17s 8d home each week, now I work 48 hrs with no half days and bring £1 13s 8d home. (I get 5/- rise when I am 16 yrs old)

28th Sept

- Very foggy until after 10am, 2 buses collide head-on near Doncaster. Afterwards it cleared up and we had our warmest day for 3 months. Britain's latest plane explodes 10,000ft up, Mr. Geoffrey De-Havillan, one of our finest test pilots is believed killed. Total people killed this month in air crashes is now 190 (8 killed today). Doncaster beat Accrington 5-0 this afternoon; they are still at the top of their league. Dad had a hard day at work distempering and whitewashing two rooms, he went to the pictures later for a change. Finished my first week of day shifts (it's a good shift when 2pm comes around). I am on nights next week. The verdicts for the Goering and Party trial will be given on Monday and Tuesday, their wives visit for the last time.

29th Sept

- Dad went to Doncaster for the afternoon out, it is the first time he has been out for a long time. He brought Mam a Guinness back (they are hard to get). A very sunny day. Bill went to church. He also went for a cycle ride this afternoon with some others, Bill said they were just riding by an orchard and some apples fell into their pockets (he came home with 17 apples).

30th Sept

- Goering and Party will be sentenced tomorrow, Hess says he has consulted the stars and says a miracle will happen; Goering and three others want to be shot. I went blackberrying this afternoon; the weather is still very warm. They have started making a film of Bruce Woodcock's home-life; it will take 3 weeks to complete. Bill went for some conkers (horse chestnuts).

1st Oct

- Dad's birthday aged 46 (Peg sent him a card). 21 leading Nazis sentenced today, the sentences are: **Sentenced to Death** - (13) Goering, Ribbentrop, Kietal, Kaltenbrunner, Rosenburg, Frank, Frick, Stiecher, Sauckel, Jodl, Seyss, Inquart, and Bormann was entenced in his absence. **Life imprisonment** - Hess, Funk, Raeder, Admiral Doenitz (10yrs), Speer (25 yrs), Von Nevrath (15 yrs), and Schirach (15 yrs). **Acquitted** - Von Papen, Schacht, and Frische. I worked my first night shift.

2nd Oct

- Those sentenced to death will be hanged on October 16th. Rossington pit goes on strike, they say that they cannot earn sufficient wages owing to bad conditions down pit. Oranges in Rossington. Electric organ blowers installed in church which means they will not need me to pump it now.

3rd Oct

- We come to an understanding with Russia at last; they have agreed to destroy Zone War Plant. 4 power pact signatures lifts iron curtain (Berlin Wednesday). Another plane crashed yesterday killing all the 39 crew and passengers (U.S. plane). The German people want to arrest the 3 acquitted men at Nuremburg for treason, they dare not leave Nuremburg.

4th Oct

- Pay day £1 13s 8d. Hess is to serve his sentence in a mental hospital. Bill and Dad went to the pictures. I found out tonight that I will get time and ¼ for working nights and time plus ¾ for Sunday. Got a paper asking me to join the railway union. Rossington strike still on until it is settled, 3,000 tons of coal will be lost each day. Dad brings home £5 for 6 shifts hard work. When the pit is to be inspected the managers are told before and they get the pit put right, dad says they even let fresh air in when the inspector goes down.

5th Oct

- I will have to cycle to work tonight as buses don't start running until 2pm. The clocks have to be put back tomorrow morning at 2am.

Rovers won again, they played Barrow and won 1-0 away. The most goals scored by a single team for over 10 years were scored by Newcastle when they won Newport 13-0 this afternoon. Set off for work at 9:05pm, arrived at 9:40pm (7 miles). There will be a meeting in Rossington picture-house tomorrow evening over the pit strike, Mr. Tom Hall, miners leader, will be there.

6th Oct

- I worked the longest hour I have ever worked this morning, 2am until 3am, it had 120 minutes in it. I knocked off at 5am instead of 6am. Still waiting for my suit which we ordered from Burton's 6 weeks ago. That is why I have not been to church for the last few weeks (7). Bill attended communion this morning but did not get to the 6pm service. Dad went to the strike meeting. I have not been to the pictures this week, that's 3/- saved.

7th Oct

- I have not been to the pictures for a week and I will not be able to go this week as I am on afters' (6/- saved). Sent crossword away to John Bull, Sent away for a book called 'The Secret of Good Letter Writing', 1/- to John Bull. Went blackberrying with Bill and got 7lbs (morning). An American long-distance plane has flown 9,500 miles non-stop, it arrived in Britain 15 minutes before schedule, it has been north over the magnetic pole, he was lost over England but was saved by radar.

8th Oct

- Mam draws £1 out of family allowance as she missed last week. I got pair of new shoes, black size 10. Bill off school with cold. Got a form for my railway uniform, I have to send my measurements in to the Y.M.O. for waistcoat, trousers, jacket, cap, and overcoat. Bill went to the pictures. It has been sunshining every day for the last week (it would be)!

9th Oct

- Got 2lbs of bananas from Ward's. The Miners Union says the men are to go back to work on Sunday. They were promised better conditions and more money. Dad says the conditions are still bad and the money is still low.

10th Oct

- I knocked three mantles off (3/-) they are very hard to get, Mam's tempers up. Bill went chestnutting, they are 4/- per lb in Doncaster and walnuts 8/- per lb.

11th Oct

- Pay day £1 13s 4d. Thought I would get extra night duty pay 12/- but have to wait until next week, it would have come in very handy as Dad only has 17/- (1 shift) to draw with going on strike last week. Dad does a lot of work for small wages. Mr. Ward sent some eggs, first time we've had some for 5 weeks, also got some oranges.

12th Oct

- I am 16 yrs old today and joined LNER union. Peg sent 2/6 and a card for birthday. Dad and Mam will give me something later as we have had a bad week. Doncaster beats Bradford City 4-3 at home, they are still top of league 3 with 18 points. 'Airborne' beaten today in the King George 5th stakes by the French horse 'Sovereign'. 'Bright News' came second, 'Airborne' came third (2 miles). Dad put 2/- on a horse 'Jupiter Island' and it came 1st at 4 to 1 so he now has 10/- to come back, that's with his own 2/-.

13th Oct

- The Nuremburg appeals have all been turned down, those sentenced to death have been praying today as it is their last Sunday (all but Rosenburg who says he won't believe in God to the end).

14th Oct

- Went to the pictures for the first time in 2 weeks. Bruce Woodcock will fight George Martin, the new French champion on November 15th.

15th Oct

- 21o prisoners at Dartmoor have gone on hunger strike following the freeing of the 250 paratroopers that were sentenced to 2 years for refusing to go on parade. Some of those at Dartmoor are on life sentences for mutiny at Northallerton a few months back, I am sure they have not done as much wrong as Hess who also has a life sentence. The hanging of Goering and Party will start at 12:01am tomorrow morning (unofficial). Rosenburg refused to turn to religion in his last hours. Grapes are now selling at 6d per ¼, they were as much as 4/- per ¼ during the war. My Grandmother sent Bill and I 21/- for birthday.

16th Oct

- Goering committed suicide at 10:30pm last night (1½ hrs before he was due to be hanged), he took poison but no-one knows where he got it from (potassium Cyanide). There are 2 theories. One is that his wife passed it to him while giving him his last kiss (through the prison bars), the second theory is that his German barber slipped it between his collar and neck. The other 10 prisoners were hanged in pairs over a period of 1hr 35 minutes. Heath murderer was hanged today. Dad applied for a job for Bill at the Co-op butchers (the boss will see about it).

17th Oct

- I can now manage the train booking without help so I will be transferred to another signal-box a week tomorrow. Queen Elizabeth sails on her maiden voyage at 2pm this afternoon; she was converted into a troop ship during the war years. Went to the pictures to see 'Burma Victory' it was very good. Duke and Duchess of Windsor's jewels stolen.

18th Oct

- Pay day £2 2s 9d with night duty. The Windsor's lost £20,000 worth of jewels (serves them right, they have only been here one week and have too much money to be careful!) Mr. Ward sent us a Rowntree's jelly (blocks). Ray had never seen one before.

19th Oct

- Doncaster Rovers beat York City 4-1 at York today, they are still top of league 3.

20th Oct

- Sunday has been the dreariest day of the week for me (for about 6 weeks) as I don't like going out with my everyday clothes on (I have had a suit ordered for about 2 months) Mam says I should go out but I don't. That is the reason I have not been to church recently.

21st Oct

- Bought a lamp and cycled to work. Bill off school again this week (he had a cough and is chestier. Mam and Dad went to Doncaster to see about my suit but they say they do not know when it will be done. Ordered 2/6 worth of fireworks, will get them tomorrow.

22nd Oct

- I got 22 fireworks from Pointer's. Bill brought wooden spoon home from night school. Mr Fawcett, my old school master left £2028 in his will (net £1096).

23rd Oct

- Dad, Bill, and I moved 4 tons of coke from in front of the church hall into the church yard in 1½ hrs. Received a book from John Bull which I sent for 2 weeks ago, they call it 'The Art of Good Letter Writing', 1/-.

24th Oct

- The painter came this morning, I was kept awake until 12pm, I am on nights.

25th Oct

- Winter seemed to come all of a sudden this morning, everything was covered with frost and very cold. Bill and I got a ton of coal in.

26th Oct

- I can't find anything to put in my diary. There is only 9 weeks left of this year and I don't think I will fill it, (this bit will help). I got soaking wet last night riding to work, the tele-girl on afters' asked me to come and relieve her at 9 o'clock so she could go to a dance. When I got there at 9pm I found that she had not been to work at all so I had wasted an hour of a lesson.

27th Oct

- I wrote a letter to my Grandmother, we have now got £4 10s in my bank. Ray now has 94 Sunday school stars (he has missed 2 Sundays this year). Three more jewel thefts have took place in the last few days. It is now known how Goering killed himself. He had the poison with his for 17 months (he kept it hidden on his body), letters were found in his left hand stating this. I am to continue working at Red Bank until a box is available.

28th Oct

- I am on afters' this week. Cycled to work, had a haircut, and bought a battery for my front lamp, haircuts are now 1/3, or 1/6 on a Saturday. Dad got a load of coal in for Mr. Roebuck (the Parson), he came and asked, he gave him 2/6. Mam says if he was a real parson he would get it in himself.

29th Oct

- [blank]

30th Oct

- Bill and Ray break up for 2 days holiday from school. Mr Meadows says he will give Dad 8/6 for getting 4 tons of coke in last Thursday (he's not got it yet). Mam has a very hard job finding something to put on my snap (6 rounds), it's nearly always jam but she managed to make me a fairly good lot today by putting some sausage meat on and it turned out alright.

31st Oct

- Started to make a garage for Ray (Xmas). Elections will be carried out all over England tomorrow for municipal Mayors etc. Completed a John Bull crossword (at work), will send it away next week.

1st Nov

- Socialites came out top in the elections (saved a few seats). I have to be at work at 6am tomorrow morning as a tele-girl (the one I relieved for an hour last week and who made a fool of me) is having the day off so I will take over Red Bank myself. I finished at 9pm and back at 6am. Pay day £1 12s 1d, I have not got my rise yet but it is in order as I work a week in hand. Bought a new battery for my rear light.

2nd Nov

- I came home at 2pm after taking over the telegraphing of a signal-box myself, as it happened I was put on the busiest morning of the busiest shift (days) and we had the most trains I'd known since I started. I managed OK (the signalman said I was very good). It was also very foggy and we had no signalmen on duty, they place detonators on the lines to act as the signals (they are explosives). The bus was late and I got there at 6:10 but that was not my fault (first time late). Dad is working Sunday double time. Doncaster Rovers draw with Darlington 1-1, I think they are still top of league 3. Mr. Meadows, the church warden brought Dad 8/6 for getting the coke in and me 10/s for my last 3 months pumping; we have decided to buy Charlie's Xmas present with it.

3rd Nov

- Ray now has 96 church stars. Today Bill and I were looking at some fireworks we had bought from Potter's. I happened to take the paper from one and found that they were the old pre-war fireworks with a new paper cover on, the old paper had ½d stamped on and the new paper had 1d (Frauds)! A former German S.S. man says he has seen Bormann (Hitler's deputy who was sentenced to death in his absence) in a city in the U.S. zone. I am on days this week.

4th Nov

- The YMO told me to report to Decoy No.1 tomorrow. Mischievous night, the nips will be on the run! Dad and Bill went to the pictures. We may get extra rations for Xmas says Strachey, we will get 2/- worth of meat extra per head, certain children 1/6 worth. Freddie Mills fights Joe Baski (who is 32lb heavier) tomorrow. I dug Mrs.

Holmes' garden over, will finish it off tomorrow, she is giving me 2/6. The lads are all gathering wood for their bonfires.

5th Nov

- It's Bonfire Night! Bill, Ray, and I have 18 fireworks to set off. Ray and I are going to the pictures first. We have no fire. Mam and Dad went to Doncaster to get a few things in hand for Xmas. Munson set some 2/6 rockets and other fireworks off. Mam and Dad ordered Charlie a wooden horse from Currie's, we have to go for it next Saturday £1 1s 9d.

6th Nov

- [blank]

7th Nov

- Foggy. I was 20 minutes late for work. Went to the pictures with Bill to see 'The Brighton Strangler'. A miner was killed by a fall at the pit today.

8th Nov

- Pay day £2 2s 9d, I have not got my rise yet. Went into Red Bank box for an hour while the girl went for wages. Cycled to work, very windy. Set of at 4:55am and got there at 5:55am. Mam sold the pram o Mrs. Griffiths for 30/-. We now have £5 1s 6d in my club. Bill has 14/6, Mam has 11/6, Dad has 5/6, and Frank has £3 10s. I get 5/- pocket money now. Bought a poppy as I got my wages.

9th Nov

- I called in at Currie's, Doncaster today as I was coming home from work. I paid 6/9 and brought Charlie's wooden horse home (put it away for his Xmas present). Doncaster Rovers beat Hull City today 4-1 (still top of the league). Dad put 1/- on a horse but it lost. Mam bought a new jumper, it is the first time she has bought herself anything for ages. Mam and Ray went to the 1st House pictures, Bill went 2nd. Mam gave Mary Morgan (a friend) 29 points for her wedding cake as she is getting married shortly. I am on nights next week. Bill and I have worked it out so as we give 8 shillings to each as Xmas presents out of our Xmas savings. Bill has saved £1 and I will put £1 too and buy 5 eight shilling presents (including Bill).

10th Nov

- Dad went down to Young's (wireless man) and bought a battery 14/2, now got wireless going. But we've not got a license yet, it's good to hear it again. Remembrance Day parade not as good as war years. Point period 5 begins today, still bread units. Bought some raffle tickets (Xmas). Sent Ray a note up the chimney to Santa Claus. Bill went to church. Mam and Dad went for a walk down the old village. Set the firework off which we were saving for Xmas.

11th Nov

- Remembrance Day. Got up at 7am. Tidied up a bit and took Mam and Dad a cup of tea up stairs. Went to the pictures with Bill to see 'Murder in Music Hall'. Bought Charles a small car (2/-), from Bill. I've had no sleep today and expect to be tired at work tonight (shift work isn't as good as it sounds). Cycled to Bessacarr to see how much a toy car was for Ray's Xmas box, I expected 5/- but it was 15/-! Bought Bill a table tennis set 6/6, Ray a money box 8½d (but will buy Ray something else). I have 8/- to spend on each.

12th Nov

- Came home from work very tired at 7:30, I have to wait until 7am for the first bus. Went to bed at 8am and got up at 6pm. Bill went to night school. The bill to keep children at school until 15yrs old will be passed in April (says wireless). Weather forecast says gales and very cold tonight so I will go to work on the bus. Bruce Woodcock fights George Martin (French) over 10 rounds on Friday. The King opened parliament today.

13th Nov

- I found out last night that the first bus runs at 6am so I finished work at 5:30am and caught it. When I got into Rossington I found it was the pit bus and so had to walk from the pit (but that is better than waiting for the 7am bus). Borrowed 1/- from club and went to the pictures. Went to bed at 7am and got up at 4pm. There is to be a statue erected in Grosvenor Square (in bronze) of President Roosevelt (10 feet high). Most of the pre-fabs and permanent houses are now occupied (the pre-fabs look alright).

14th Nov

- It's rained ever since last night. Mam sold 20 clothing coupons to Mary Morgan (on the quiet) as she is getting married a fortnight on Friday (she sold them for £1). Snow in Scotland. I caught the 6am bus and in bed for 6:30am, got up at 5:30pm.

15th Nov

- Pay day £2 14s 5d, got my rise 5/- and 5/- for each of the 3 weeks that I missed. Dad brought £8 home with rent paid, he worked Sunday last week. Bruce Woodcock (Don) knocked out George Martin (France) in the 3rd round at Belle Vue (Manchester) tonight. His next fight is on December 17th against Olle Tandeburg (Sweden) or Joe Baksi (U.S.) Mam gave me 10s pocket money for bringing my extra rises home. Bought some toothpaste from a shop (when I asked the price she said it has 1/- stamped on it but that it was 1/3, I paid).

16th Nov

- Mam and Dad went to Doncaster and bought Ray a new suit for £2 5s 5d. Doncaster Rovers beat Gateshead 3-1 away (still top of league 3). Bill went to the pictures. Went to bed at 7:30am and got up at 5pm. Last race in the season (Gordon Richards is the champion with over 200 wins this year). Cycled to work (nights). Charlie got his first pair of trousers with braces (8/6).

17th Nov

- Bill attended 9:30am communion and 6:30pm evensong. Ray attended Sunday school. I applied for Red Bank signal-box (the first boy taught) at work this morning at work. Went to bed at 7am and got up at 2pm (worked last night). I am on afternoons next week. Wrote letter to Peg. We had £10 14s wages this week (with my own) the biggest we have ever had. Mam and Dad went to Doncaster yesterday, now we only have 30/- left and not much to show for it (Ray's new suit).

18th Nov

- Went to Doncaster at 12 o'clock and had a look around the shops. I saw a gun (pistol) 5/6, a car (wind-up) 3/4½, I will take 10/- with me tomorrow and buy them for Ray's Xmas present (Bill is helping to pay). Mam and Dad went to the Gaumont to see 'Concerto', they say it was one of the best pictures they have seen. We are still having very bad weather (wind and rain today). Big bus strike in Manchester, 500,000 people walk to work as 5,000 conductors and drivers go on strike. The strike is over one man being sacked for dangerous driving.

19th Nov

- Took a pound note to Doncaster to buy the gun and car but when I got there the shopkeeper said that the 2 in the window are only for show and they haven't got any until the next lot come in. I bought Charlie a tennis ball for 2/6. I got a letter from the YMO which says that I have got Red Bank signal-box permanently from the 23rd November. They are sacking the girls!

20th Nov

- Les Young, wireless man came and asked if Mam and Bill would work in his shop starting at 15/- per week. Man says she would see when Dad comes in at 12 o'clock. If Bill takes the job we will get his family allowance stopped (5/-) and he will want 5/- pocket money so I say wait for a better job. (Not very neat but I'm in a hurry. Bill has taken the job with Les Young (wireless man) and starts tomorrow at 15/- per week.

21st Nov

- Raymond's birthday aged 7yrs. Bill starts his new job at the wireless shop. When I reckoned my club up today I was 6/6 in hand (I had not been reckoning the money which is in the savings tin). We now have £5 15s 6d saved in my club. It was pouring with rain yesterday and it's very windy today. The signalman let me come home early (6:35) so I caught the 7pm bus and went to the pictures to see 'The Body Snatcher'.

22nd Nov

- No-one has sent Ray anything for his birthday yet. Mam bought him a suit, 2 bars of chocolate, and a ¼ of caramels; I bought him a money box. I was told at work this afternoon that I have to go to work at 6am to Decoy No. 1 (the box I have just learned) to relieve the tele-girl who is having the day off. I finished work at 7:40pm. Pay day £1 17s

1d. The union collector came and took 2/8 of that. It has been raining and raining the whole of the last week and floods have been reported from all over England (we never get flooded in Rossington).

23rd Nov

- Got up at 4:15am not feeling too well. (Still Raining). Went to work with Tom Hayes (another Rossington tele-lad), had a fairly busy shift. Got home at 3:15pm still feeling bad (I didn't eat all my snap) Sat by the fire until 5 o'clock (didn't move) and then went to bed. Bill brings his first wage home, 7/6 for 3 days. Mam says she will give him 6d per shift so that's 3 bob a week he will get for himself. (I am writing all this on Tuesday the 26th). Doncaster Rovers beta Hartlepool 5-1, still topping the league, attendance 14,000 at home. Doncaster boys also won their game against Barnsley 5-1.

24th Nov

- Bill attended 6:30pm evensong, he was too late for communion (the Bishop of Sheffield took the communion service). Ray now has 100 Sunday school stars. It's not finished raining yet, it's been on for over a week.

25th Nov

- I start permanent job at Red Bank today (afters'). Caught the 10:45pm bus and was home at 11:15pm. Bill has sold one 1d spoke at work today. There is a big court case now going on over Mrs. Titcher treating one of her children cruelly (a little girl 8yrs old), she has burned her feet and punched her nose, and she always kept her in a room away from the others.

26th Nov

- Bill's half day, he took Mam to Doncaster to do a bit of Xmas shopping. They bought Ray a gun for 7/6, a ship for 1/6, and a plane for 1/6. He bought himself a jigsaw. We have now spent £1 4s 2½d of the £2 we are spending on presents (8/- each). Mam bought Dad a new cap which he needed. Bill also called in at the labour exchange. I caught the 10:45 bus home. Thousands of U.S. miners are on strike.

27th Nov

- Mrs. Titcher was yesterday sentenced to 2 years imprisonment for cruelty and neglect and her husband got 6 months for neglect. England beat Holland 8-2 at Huddersfield today. This afternoon the signalman told me to catch a trackless (bus) to the racecourse, he said I might catch the 10:15 Rossington bus that way so I caught the tram and was at the racecourse at 10:15 but the Rossington bus would not stop. I was just walking a little further along when a car stopped and he asked if I wanted a lift. I got out of the car and caught the 10:30pm bus at Ellers road (3½d).

28th Nov

- 28 days to Xmas. The naval evacuation of the Nile was completed yesterday; the army will be out in 4 months. Received a letter from Peg. Mrs. Collins, the lady where she works has been to Paris for a week so Peg had another week's holiday. I caught the 10:30 bus home.

29th Nov

- Pay day £2 9s 3d (night duty). We now have £6 15s 6d in the club between us. Bill has £1, Mam has 16/-, Dad has 11/6, and I have £4 8s 0d. Bill's shop is now getting a few more customers; he says he's taken over £4 today. The test match starts in Australia, Don Bradman is playing for Aussie and Len Hutton is our captain. Australia made a great start, Don Bradman and A.L. Hasset are still in and have 162 runs.

30th Nov

- Mr. Churchill is 72 yrs old today. I got a letter from Burton's (tailors) asking me to call in for my new suit as it is finished (we have waited about 5 months). Brian Sellers, reporting from Australia says the Australians can't lose now with their Brisbane record, 595 for 5. We got Bradman out today (he knocked 187) and yesterday he was 162 not out. Bradman and Hasset made a stand of 276. Bill brings his first full wage home, 15/-. Doncaster draws against Accrington Stanley 2-2 in the first round of the cup.

1st Dec

- The best news we have had for a long time today, Dad has won the football sweep with no sharers!! £8 - his team was Dundee, he has got 11 goals in 3 week's; it is the most we have ever won. Ray attended Sunday school. America is now making Atom bombs 6 times as powerful as the first. Doncaster plays a return match with Accrington on Wednesday. I now have to write 10 lines a day for the rest of the month or I will not fill my diary. Mam drew £1 out of my club (she now has 10/- left.

2nd Dec

- Days this week. Had a busy morning. Drew £1 5s out of the school bank which leaves 15/- left in. £2 3s 4d in the Midland bank and 10/- in my tin. All together £3 8s 0d has been drawn out for Xmas. Presents: Mam - £1 (left 10/- in). Bill - £1. And I drew out £1 8s and left £2 in. Dad brought £8 football sweep money home and gave it to Mam. England got the rest of Australia out today, their team scored 645 all out (the last 5 were out in 1 hour). Sellers says a draw is likely (but Bradman and Len Hutton was out for 21). Play was stopped today owing to strong light. Got some curtaining (calico) from Peck's, 8 yds £1 2s (16 coupons).

3rd Dec

- Met Bill at the bus stand in Waterdale and went shopping for some Xmas presents but all we bought was a tobacco pouch for Dad (8/6), and a Xmas card. Mam and Dad called into Burton's and paid the remaining £2 15s 0d off my suit, I collected it this afternoon. Dad also paid what was still owed on the bed (which has been on order for about 2 months). The price is £9 7s 0d. We bought a mirror (10" x 12") for 8/6, Ray got some boots 11/-, Bill and I had a milkshake each (6d each) and went into the picture house to see 'Piccadilly Incident'. Bill's half day. There has been 8 inches of snow in some parts of Yorkshire; we saw snow on the expresses coming from the north.

4th Dec

- Doncaster Rovers won their match against Accrington 5-0 in the first round for the cup. Mr. Ward sold us some Xmas apples. When Bill started at Mr. Young's he said he would get Bill an electric fire for inside the shop, he has not got it yet and Bill is very cold sitting there all day. 22 passengers were injured when the Queen Elizabeth ran into a westerly gale on Monday (85,000 tonnes). Bruce Woodcock fight Nisse Anderson the Swede on December 17th. We have £1 left out of Dad's £8 winnings (bed, suit, boots, mirror, and different things). Bill and I went to the pictures to see 'Booked on Suspicion'.

5th Dec

- Australia has won the first test match by 1 inning and 332 runs (we scored 199). Sellers said there is no disgrace in losing this first test as we had all the bad luck (rain). There is 4 more test matches left to play (Sellers said England will win the next). Bill sold more things today than any other day since he started, he took £6 17s 0d, had a very busy morning. Very frosty. We've had 2 lots of carol singers tonight (went to bed at 6:30pm). Rossington shops are now selling Xmas apples. Union fined Lewis £877,500. Lewis is the leader of the U.S. soft coal miners. His case has been on for a week. Doncaster racecourse is now all ready for tomorrow.

6th Dec

- Pay day £1 17s 1d. The 2 day national hunt meeting starts today. The hunt course is said to be the best in the north, there has not been a hunt meeting at Doncaster for 35 years. Dad got 29/ 1¾ per shift last week (he only got 4 in). America's nationwide coal strike has stopped. Britain's order from U.S. and delay the end of B.U's, the ration may even be cut. Took Ray's glasses to be repaired (Rayner's). Doncaster Rovers play Lincoln City tomorrow at Lincoln. I slept in the new bed last night (comfortable).

7th Dec

- Very foggy and frosty this morning (early). Dad took Ray to Doncaster to see Santa but they were closed. Mam has not been very well this week. Changing Bread Units for points ends today (but you can still change points for B.U's.) Last day of point period 5. Got some apples (2lbs), 3 grapefruit, and 2 tangerine oranges from Cunar's (greengrocer). Doncaster Rovers won their game against Lincoln away 5-3. Bill's pay day 15/-.

8th Dec

- Ray is getting wise about Santa Claus, he is looking around for toys (one of the nips has told him that there isn't a Santa). I finished work yesterday afternoon until 10pm on Monday night. The miners are to get Xmas day and Boxing day holiday with pay (£1 for each) on condition that they have worked at least one day this year. I will be on day shift for Xmas week. Dad went to church at 6:30pm. I tried my new suit on, it fits perfectly (navy blue).

9th Dec

- Night shift. Raining this morning as Bill and I left. I often wish I was back at school. There is only Ray at school at the moment. 124 people were killed when a 15 storey building in U.S. caught fire on Saturday. The U.S. coal strike has ended (it may save our cut in bacon ration). Went to the pictures to see 'The Racket Man' (took Ray and Bill). Big pit explosion at Whitehaven under-sea pit, many men killed.

10th Dec

- Very frosty as I came home this morning (caught 7am bus). Bill's half day, he went to the labour exchange to get his unemployment card. Britain's new jet Flying Wing will make its test flight soon (Armstrong). There was a half hour electricity cut this morning after an appeal failed just before the 8am news. 14 men are now known to have been killed in the Whitehaven pit explosion. Went to bed at 8am and got up at 4pm.

11th Dec

- Last night when I went down to catch the 9 o'clock bus I found that they had stopped running at 6:30pm, I waited until 9:45 to see if any workers buses would turn up but they didn't (although the fog was not very bad in Rossington, visibility was only 5 yds on the north road. My front cycle light was bad so I went home and missed my first shift; other LNER men went home also. Raining very fast this morning.

12th Dec

- The King celebrated his 10th year on the throne on Tuesday. Very frosty early this morning as I caught the 7am bus home. The second test match starts in Australia tomorrow. Pasted some pictures in my diary. Went to bed at 8am and got up at 6pm. Bible films are now being made in the U.S. Had fish and chips for supper. Bruce Woodcock said he is getting married soon but he is keeping the date a secret.

13th Dec

- Hammond (England Captain) won the toss this morning and decided to bat first, we are only 219 for 8 up to press (first day). Bought a new rear light (2/5). There are rumours that the bacon ration will be cut on January 7th. Mam bought Ray a lotto set (3/11) toward his Xmas presents. Pay day £1 17s 1d. Dad bought some buns from the pit, they taste like soap, Ray found a piece of string 6" long in his! Doncaster Rovers play Oldham tomorrow away. Went to bed at 8:50am until 2pm and then again 6pm until 8pm.

14th Dec

- Foggy this morning. The English team are all out for 265, Australia has lost 1 wicket for 29 runs and play was stopped today owing to bad light. Doncaster Rovers beat Oldham away in the 2nd round for the cup. Bill's pay day 15/-. Got a Xmas cake for 5/6, 1lb of mincemeat, a lb tin of peaches, and dried fruit. He's got no Xmas puddings and we can't have any suet so we look like being without one. I cycled to work. Bill went to the pictures. Disarmament plans were passed today by UNO. All letters and parcels must be posted before December 18th to reach by Christmas.

15th Dec

- Snow and very cold (maybe below freezing point) is forecast on the 6:00pm news. Went to bed at 10am and got up at 2:30pm. Bill missed church again this week. Ray got his new star card. Doncaster Rovers play Portsmouth at home in the 3rd round of the cup on Saturday 21st. Today has been the coldest day of winter so far. Dad brought a clock from Marshes for Mam to see but she says she will wait for a new one.

16th Dec

- Afternoon shift. Very cold this morning and it has been snowing on and off all day but it did not settle. Bought 2lbs of sweets and chocolate to put away for Xmas. Mam baked Ray a cake to take to school as it is his party day tomorrow. Dad slept in for work. Australia are only 4 runs behind us (157) and still have 6 wickets standing (2nd test).

17th Dec

- Dad had a bit of luck yesterday when one of his Xmas draw raffle tickets came up, it just says prize on the ticket so we don't know what it is until we get it. Bruce Woodcock won his fight against the Swede. Nisse Anderson threw in the towel in the third round. The prize Dad won yesterday turned out to be 10/- when Bill went down to get it. Mam and Dad went to Doncaster to buy some presents (bought Peg a hand mirror 26/-).

18th Dec

- Bruce Woodcock the Doncaster boxer gets married tomorrow. Got a pack of playing cards from Cook's (4/6) for Xmas. I had my hair cut. Today is supposed to be the last day for posting parcels for Xmas but we haven't posted any yet. Doncaster Rovers play Rotherham on Saturday at home.

19th Dec

- Australia has won the 2nd test match. Bought Bill a box of 3 darts. Uncle Charlie and Kate sent us an ornament for Xmas (a pot choir boy). Bruce Woodcock is married.

20th Dec

- Pay day £1 17s 6d. Very cold and frosty. The miners get their five day week starting next May.

21st Dec

- Doncaster Rovers draw with Rotherham, 1-1. Mam baked our Xmas cakes (2). Peg sent us our Xmas parcels, Mam - Pinafore, Dad - 1 oz of Bruno, Bill - a pen-knife and book, Charlie - a farm-yard set and skittles, Ray - big story book, a jigsaw, and small books, and me - a brush and comb in a case. Bill's pay day 15/-. I found out today that I get Xmas day and Boxing day as holiday.

22nd Dec

- Big earthquake in Japan, over 1000 people killed (1 British soldier). Iced Mam's cakes, I made the first lot too thin and it spoiled. Set the toys and sweets out for Xmas. Ray gets his Sunday school prize next Sunday.

23rd Dec

- Day shift 6am. I was up at 3:30am this morning as our clock had stopped so I went for the time. Gave Mam 10/- 3 weeks ago but she has not yet got herself an Xmas present. Rained all day and colder weather is forecast for Xmas. We are all hoping for a white Christmas! Had a busy day up to 11 o'clock then we slackened off. I went into a shop today to price a bottle of port, I took 10/- but it was £1 12s (I thought they were 9/-).

24th Dec

- The LNER paid wages out today instead of Friday £2 1s 2d as I had a shift off the week before last. Bill has to work his half day said Mr. Young so as to get his Xmas holiday. Had a walk around Doncaster, it was crowded. Bought 5 tangerine oranges (1/3), a tube of Pepsodent toothpaste (1/3), and 3 drinking glasses (9d each). Met Mam, Dad, Ray, and Charlie getting the last few things in for Xmas, Dad won't show me the presents he's bought until tomorrow. Went to bed at 8pm, this is the first Xmas eve for a long time that I haven't stopped up to get out the presents.

25th Dec 1946

- **CHRISTMAS DAY**. Dad, Bill, and I get Christmas day and Boxing Day as holiday. Dad (all miners) gets his first Xmas day holiday with pay without conditions. Ray gets 2 weeks holiday from the 20th December. We haven't got a turkey or anything like that, there are plenty about but they are much too expensive for us. We managed to get a bit of pork but only 2 shillings worth (it was a taste). We have 1 Xmas pudding, 3 iced cakes, a large tin of peaches, jelly (blackcurrant), and plenty of custards. Mam baked some mince pies this afternoon so we all had a very good Xmas dinner and tea. Ray got a cannon gun, 3 story books (2 from Peg), a lotto game, 2 jigsaws (1 from Peg), a plastic ship and aeroplane, a box of paints and painting book, a tennis ball, and other small toys, he also had apples, oranges, sweets, and chocolate. Charlie got a wooden horse, a farmyard set, skittles (from Peg), a picture book, and engine, he also had sweets etc. Bill got boots, table tennis, scarf, tie, darts, book (from Peg), jigsaw, pen-knife, and sweets etc. Dad got a tobacco pouch, 1oz of Bruno, a handkerchief, 10/-, and sweets etc. Mam got a pinafore (from Peg), a bottle of Vironita, 2 bottles of Guinness, and sweets etc. Frank got a pair of black shoes, a scarf, a tie, hair oil, and sweets etc. We all stopped at home. We have all had a very happy Xmas.

26th Dec

- Got up at 8:30am (I went to bed after 12 last night). Bill and I went to the Gaumont in Doncaster, there were carol singers and the organ was played. The picture was very good. I went out in my new suit for the first time and also put my new shoes and scarf on. Bill and Ray tried to get into the Rossington pictures after we came from the Doncaster pictures but they were full. Doncaster Rovers beat Wrexham 5-0 at home. Tennis table ball got burnt.

27th Dec

- No pay today as I got aid on Tuesday. Very busy this morning. The clock stopped at 1am this morning so I had to lay awake waiting for the buzzer to go and I managed to get up alright. Dad went to work last night, he said there was only 5 men out of the 50 men that worked on his stall that turned up. Mam gave the milk girl 2/- for Xmas and the 3 paper lads 6d each. Mr Matthewman (a traveller) didn't bring Charlie his usual sweets and as soon as he went out he screamed.

28th Dec

- Doncaster Rovers won their match against Rochdale (away) 3-2, they are still top of league 3. Ray bought a new table tennis ball from the market for 6d yesterday as he knocked the other one into the fire on Thursday.

29th Dec

- Raymond was presented with the first prize today for regular attendance at Sunday school, he had over 100 stars. His prize was a story book called 'Photobus'. Bill started church again after 4 weeks absence. The next Australia V England test match starts on January 1st if Australia wins this they will win the ashes. Bruce Woodcock starts training for his fight against Baski (U.S.) tomorrow.

30th Dec

- Night shift. Took Ray to the Gaumont to see 'Great Expectations' by Charles Dickens. There was a train crash in Doncaster station just after 11am this morning and 20 to 25 people were injured (an express crashed into a standing train).

31st Dec

- Bill gets New Years Day as holiday (but he's had to work his half day to get it). Tonight at 12 o'clock I shall book the New Year at work (as I am on nights). No-one is stopping up to let the New Year in, I will let it in at 7:30am. Dad will get double pay if he works New Years Day.

The end of my 1946 diary - 86 pages - 2408 lines - by Frank Worsdale.

Post script.

- From Mam and Dad, to Frank, Christmas 1945 – No apples, oranges, or any other fruit this Christmas, Turkeys and Fowls are at black-market prices, also toys and books (6 skittles and ball costs 8/6). You can't get a toy worth looking at under 5/-. We dropped in lucky as Dad won 2 rabbits in 3d raffle at the Royal (pub), we had a small cockerel given, had 2 iced cakes, 2 xmas puddings, a jelly, and a blancmange. Ray had school party and is having party at church next Friday. I bought Dad a pipe (3/6) and Mam 2 pinafores (5/6 &3/6). I bought Ray a cowboy set (4/10½), a tin-tin game (2/-) and tiddley winks (1/6). We all had a fairly good Xmas (it was not a bit cold on Xmas day). I got £2/14/- tips at Greens shop where I work (extra tips come to £3/4/-).

THE END

DONCASTER HISTORY

Edited and compiled by Symeon M Waller.

Made in the USA
Charleston, SC
26 October 2012